W9-AFL-324

ACCIDENTS OF INFLUENCE

SUNY Series in Modern Jewish Literature and Culture
Sarah Blacher Cohen

Also by Norma Rosen

John and Anzia: An American Romance
At the Center
Touching Evil
Green
Joy to Levine!

ACCIDENTS OF INFLUENCE

Writing as a Woman and

a Jew in America

NORMA ROSEN

State University
of New York
Press

MIDDLEBURY COLLEGE LIBRARY

The following essays appeared in the *New York Times* (some titles slightly altered): "Low Thoughts Among the High-Minded," "Sons and Mothers," "Baby-Making," "Child-Abuse," "The World's First Crop," "Her Price Above Rubies," "Sometimes I Feel Like a Siblingless Child," "An Immoral Tale," "William Faulkner and the Art of Ruthlessness," "The Luck of the Trip," "Wadja Geffa Christmas, Li'l Boy?" "Reclaiming," "The Bird Has No Wings," "Hunting Metaphors and Nazis," "Writers? Women?" "The Holocaust and the American-Jewish Novelist" appeared in *Midstream*. "Simone Well—A Dissenting View" appeared initially in *Ms.* and in expanded form in *Midstream*, the version used here. "The Second Life of Holocaust Imagery" appeared initially in *Witness* and in expanded form in *Midstream*, the version used here. "The Literature of Contempt" appeared in *Present Tense*. The following appeared in *Congress Monthly*: "The Fate of Anne Frank's Diary," "Bernard Malamud and the Accidents of Influence," "On T. S. Eliot: Geniuses and Anti-Semites," "I Had the Distinct Impression Death Was Jewish," "Norman Mailer's Holocaust-Poisoned Jews," "Friday Night Fever." "On the Dearth of Female Intellectuals" appeared in *PEN Newsletter*. "Minority Writers and the American Mainstream: Telling Stories in the Houses We Create," appeared in *Confrontations*. "On Living in Two Cultures" appeared in *Response*. "Justice for Jonah" appeared in *Congregation: Contemporary Writers Read the Jewish Bible,* published by Harcourt Brace Jovanovich. "Notes Toward a Holocaust Fiction" appeared in *Testimony,* ed. David Rosenberg, published by Times Books.

Published by
State University of New York Press, Albany

© 1992 Norma Gangel Rosen

All rights reserved

Printed in the United States of America

No part of this book may be used or reproduced
in any manner whatsoever without written permission
except in the case of brief quotations embodied in
critical articles and reviews.

For information, address State University of New York
Press, State University Plaza, Albany, N.Y., 12246

Rosen, Norma.
    Accidents of influence : writing as a woman and a Jew in America / by
Norma Rosen.
        p. cm.
    ISBN 0-7914-1091-9 (alk. paper) " $34.50. — ISBN 0-7914-1092-7
(pbk. : alk paper) : $10.95
    I. Title.
PS3568.077A66   1992
814'.54—dc20   91-29320
                                                                          CIP

10 9 8 7 6 5 4 3 2 1

for
LUCY DAWIDOWITZ
1915–1990
historian of the Holocaust
loving friend and rigorous challenger

CONTENTS

FOREWORD

Though I began to publish fiction in 1959, it was not until 1973 that I risked my first foray into direct statement, unprotected by masks of fictional characters and voices. I have left these essays and short pieces as they originally appeared except for changes to omit duplications of reference or to clarify the intention of the writing, but without bringing them up to date with books or opinions that arrived at a later time. And without, also, mitigating extravagances of younger days. Did I really want, as in one despairing essay of twenty years ago, to compare the medieval blood libel against Jews with Orthodox Judaism's barring and isolating of women from ritual observance? I might not use such language now, but feel no better disposed toward either ancient insult carried forward to a presumed modernity. Sometimes I'm as moved to rail against modernity for truckling to transience as against orthodoxies for intransigence.

In 1976 I wrote about a collection of letters of an assimilated German half-Jew, Peter Schwiefert, who, in the hell of the Holocaust era in which he perished, resolved the wholeness of his identity. This remarkable act of reclamation of a lost work of poetry and truth was accomplished by its editor, the then-unknown-to-America Claude Lanzmann. A decade later, *Shoah,* Lanzmann's film documentary of surviving Holocaust victims, their tormentors, and their witnesses, burst upon our consciousness. Never have I seen the works linked, but I believe these two categories of the murdered—the lonely, fleeing individual and the abandoned, enslaved multitude—belong together.

Leaving the essays more or less as they are makes it possible to keep faith with the journey of discovery that nonfiction writing can be. In that sense, many of the essays make up a memoir as well, an account of persons, places and ideas visited and lived with in the mind. This memoir-journey has taken me through examinations of my role as a post-Holocaust writer, a woman, and a Jew in America.

Some of the essays collected here surprise me with their heaped-up wrath. I think of myself as peaceable. A way to account to myself for this tone is by acknowledging that I have what has come to be called (not often with approval) a Holocaust mentality. And so, for example, I have dealt with Norman Mailer's penchant for turning his own idealism into some messianic worldview of the moment, this time one achieved at the expense of Jews, whom he libels as too Holocaust-poisoned to join the visionary company.

The view that shapes this epithet, Holocaust mentality, contends that though the Holocaust may be the central event of our time, there is something skewed, at best awkward, in allowing it to be one's mean-all and measure. When I consider how various and beautiful life on its good days can be, I feel inclined to concur in this view myself, and want to add only that I would not have chosen such a way of responding if I could have avoided it.

Others may have had an easier time of letting go of that mentality, at least in print. One of the essays here is called "Notes Toward a Holocaust Fiction." It speaks of writers who take "working vacations" from the Holocaust, and of the Nobel-prize-winning Polish poet, Czeslaw Milosz, who writes of the need in creative life to let go of old selves and take on new ones so as not to remain "magnetized by the sight of evil perpetrated in our lifetime." For the Jewish writer, these words collide with the injunction: *Zakhor.* Remember.

Following the publication of a series of my essays in the "Hers" column of the *New York Times,* an editor solicited information from me about interests and experiences that might lead to a nonfiction book. I startled myself and him by blurting, "I am married to a man whose parents were killed in the Holocaust." After a moment he replied politely that that, after all, was my husband's story to tell, not mine.

I felt rebuked, a wife who puts on a husband's penumbra, a chameleon-female who takes on color from male concerns like the woman in Chekhov's "The Darling." If that jolt did not stop or shut me up it's because I've always known that my husband's story is his, in the eye of that annihilating storm, while mine is at the edges, in the guilt and confusion of American safety, in the tension of connection and separation, in the longing for a culture I never experienced and in the repudiation of it by everything I was raised to be.

Outsider, latecomer, sheltered agonizer, I once incurred the wrath of someone else who was Holocaust-obsessed in his own way. Holocaust infighting is one more black Jewish joke, the scandalous horror of the wounded hitting one another over the head with their crutches. After publication of "The Holocaust and the American-Jewish Novelist," a letter appeared to protest that when describing my first encounters with the Holocaust through certain readings, I had omitted the work of a survivor whose name has become synonymous with Holocaust writing. No intended slight on my part, this was mere honesty about the incomplete and patchwork-y way in which sheltered Americans like myself had come to know the subject. Seized with passionate intensity, the writer attacked in Latin: "Quod licet jovi, non licet bovi." Cattle aren't allowed to do what gods can, so hands off the subject if you are neither historian nor scholar, and not a survivor, either. My answer seems to me the most banal of truths: the Holocaust is a wound sustained by Jews and by the world; it is not an exclusive "field of study," nor do we come to our consciousness of it by way of long lists of assigned reading. That reading certainly is necessary for our precise knowledge, and precise knowledge is our task. But "consciousness," an alerting of soul and mind to empathy, may originate in less predictable ways.

In discussions with my late friend, Lucy Dawidowicz, whose staggering work, *The War Against the Jews,* is dedicated to exact, entire documenting of the catastrophe, I felt I understood her stringent professional historian's impatience with certain Holocaust survivor accounts. Hers was a point of view that sought to put evidence into the context of the whole, and survivors sometimes know nothing but their individual pain. But the sheltered American's route to awakening is another matter. When it comes to reading, a random "sliver of that darkness," as I wrote elsewhere, may be enough to sting the soul to Holocaust consciousness. Then the reading, never-ending, goes on.

Turning to the grand world of letters is not reassuring. There one finds in the shaping utterances of thinkers and poets of our time—T. S. Eliot, Paul de Man, Simone Weil—blatantly anti-

Semitic sentiments that eerily echo one another, and whose main thrust is that the disappearance of Jews (at a time when Jews were being brutally made to disappear) would be no loss to Western civilization. Addressing these writers and their ideas, I find the shock of their pronouncements undiminished each time I encounter them.

Such is the framework of part one of this collection, "A Holocaust Mentality." It is also the basis of the human struggles of part two, "Life Notes," which tacitly asks the question: Is it possible to live with renewed psychological belief (faith, some call it) in a world whose principles of justice and compassion failed during the Holocaust? We have snatched those principles back from a collapsed civilization and knocked them together again. What to Nietszche was the empty spectacle of "the eternal return" appears to be for us the only road: the repeated, exhausting, disappointing, life-giving labor of building up a principled existence.

In *The Sayings of the Fathers*, Rabbi Tarphon (First Century B.C.E.) is famously quoted: "You are not obliged to finish the task, neither are you free to desist from it." Now we must add: Nor are you freed from beginning the task again after it has been smashed to pieces.

Friendship, education, sex-and-society, the labors of artists, family needs in conflict with work, response to violence physical or mental, to contradictions in religious observance—these make up some of the subject of "Life Notes," quotidian encounters struggling (not always successfully; beginning the task but not completing it) for moral ground in our own era that follows the darkest times history has to offer.

The closing "Celebrations" is limited to two, a number distinctly diminished from neighboring groups. What, only two celebrations, no more?

I feel bound to state that I have celebrated other occasions in private; and in print with my children, Anna and Jonathan, have collaborated on a picture book called *A Family Passover*, published by The Jewish Publication Society. Still, couldn't I have managed to find a few other holiday/ritual occasions to write about? "Not yet," was Franz Rosenzweig's reply when asked about his moving further along in Jewish observance. Many things are possible, but not just yet.

That these celebration/observances are largely familial probably says something about the way I approach this part of the journey. It brings me, if not exactly full circle, then I hope at least to some recognizable point of departure in the matter of being a woman and a Jew who writes in an America always gallant but on the whole stunningly indifferent to both.

1. A Holocaust Mentality

The Holocaust and the American-Jewish Novelist

I was surprised to find myself asked to be a speaker at a conference on Holocaust writing. The reason I was asked, I was told, was because I was one of the very few American fiction writers to have treated the subject.

I began to wonder why. Why so few had written, and why this conference, for which a lone writer had to be searched out and tapped.

From there it was a short step to wondering about who had been writing what in America and how, and by what path one might travel from one set of questions to another. Finally there emerged a whole curve of questions upon which I bridged my way.

A backward and painful journey. First, back to the moment or extension of moments when the revelation of the Holocaust is taken into one's being—flesh-and-spirit-altering. Then to the years during which the novel, *Touching Evil*, was painfully written, and then to the responses, some of which were also painful because the novel was praised for what was not intended—for a depiction merely of the evil in everyday life.

In order to talk about writing about the Holocaust as an American, I have to think back also to what it felt like to write fiction as a Jew in America when I first began, and about what the so-called genre of the Jewish novel has been—and what it did and did not make available to someone who wanted to write about the Holocaust.

As to who is speaking, who is "I," the answer is that it is someone who looked into Jewish history for the first time through the burnt opening of the Holocaust.

Quickly and inadequately, I must touch also on what it means to be a fiction writer, and how that affects the fate of any subject the fiction writer writes about.

This essay is in some ways itself emblem and warning about this last matter. It is not well rounded or nicely balanced, and comes to few conclusions.

True enough, it's divided into two parts—the first is large and bulky, the second part is a ridiculous wisp, like a bobbed tail on a big dog.

The trouble lies with the best and the worst aspects of what it means to be a fiction writer. Fiction writers rely on ambiguity; they put their ideas forward behind the protection of characters' masks. Fiction writers find this congenial, not because they are afraid to speak the truth, but because they find truth to be slippery—or to put it more elegantly, truth is in the dialectic itself, in the interplay of ideas; ideas moreover that in life never express themselves purely but are always modified, sometimes grotesquely, sometimes nobly, by human behavior.

In short, whenever I must come right out and make straightforward statements about the way things are, without the aid of the ambiguities of fiction, without the inconsistent behavior of characters who act like real people, I worry. I feel I may, by the logic of thought, by the inexorable march of relevant word after relevant word, be trapped into saying something that sounds rhetorically right, but that I will discover, the next time I sit down to write a piece of fiction, to be utterly wrong.

As you see, my opinion of ideas in themselves is so low that I will go to any length to discredit them. Not only do I maintain that ideas in themselves don't exist in this world; I also say that they exist in a very bad form.

But perhaps, instead of idea, what I really mean is ideology? Idea, myth, blind adherence (an idolatry of ideas)—these things are, and ought to be, kept separate from each other but have been shaken up together so that it is almost impossible now to keep them apart.

Hence my opinion that ideas are like dogs. They can be trained to do anything. Even to deny themselves. The art of fiction, on the other hand, is like a cat. It cannot be trained to betray its nature.

For now, I must be both dog and cat. And so my words are bound to fight with each other. The best I can do about this is to promise at least not to conceal the quarrel from you.

How many Jews can a Jew speak for? Few enough. When those Jews are writers, even fewer.

Mostly I speak for myself, my own experience.

I have not read every Jewish writer. Some of them I have not had time to read. Some I have not wanted to read. But I have the sense of an ambiance. If for no other reason, though there are other reasons, I would have it because critical opinion reflects the notion that there is a genre of writing in America that is Jewish.

But that is not the same as writing as a Jew in America.

Is writing as a Jew in America so different from writing as not a Jew in America? Before you turn away from the question, because it is so simpleminded—you will immediately know that of course it's different, and day by day events make it clear that it is different—let me quickly tell you my feeling that for many years, and for many people—and I am one of the people—it has been the same.

Think for a moment of what it is that the renaissance of the black artist in this country springs from: the black artist has tried to make a commitment, a covenant, as it were, out of genetic accident—the accident of being born black. They have said, these black artists, to themselves and to the world, that to be born black is not an accident, but rather a special dimension of soul. And the special dimension comes not from what the black now calls his "diaspora" experience—that is, humiliation, subjugation in every land that is not Africa—but rather a mystical ethos of blackness.

Isn't this the opposite of what has been the case with most Jewish writers? They have tried to subsume the commitment to covenant within the accident of birth: "I happen to be born Jewish," the writer says, "there is only this accident of birth. Otherwise I bleed, love, hunger, die, and respond to art like all my human brothers and sisters."

When Graham Greene in *The Heart of the Matter* has Scobie, a Catholic, commit adultery and then suicide, the special dimension of pain comes from the acknowledgment that it is, precisely, a Catholic who commits these acts.

Seldom have Jews in contemporary literature looked at their defection from ethical behavior and seen themselves as having fallen from their place as part of a "kingdom of priests."

Saul Bellow, in a fascinating essay written in the early sixties, speaks of the first Jewish writers in America, their scenes of ghetto life in Poland and Russia.

"They tended," he tells us, "to idealize it, to cover it up in prayer shawls and phylacteries and Sabbath sentiment, the Seder, the matchmaking, the marriage canopy; for sadness the Kaddish, for amusement the schnorrer, for admiration the bearded scholar. Jewish literature and art have sentimentalized and sweetened the ghetto; their pleasing pictures are far less interesting of course than the real thing."

He goes on to make a plea for "maintaining the distinction between public relations and art."

Yet, for a long while after that period, no one was worrying much about public relations for the Jew.

No need to rehearse here the stages of Jewish writing in America since those early pictures of ghetto life.

Arthur Miller's first published novel (and as far as I know his only novel) was *Focus*.

Here is a précis of the book, quoted from the 1945 Library Journal: "An American of English descent named Newman begins to wear glasses, from then on is mistaken for a Jew and becomes the victim of anti-Semitic persecution."

And here is an excerpt from something called "The Weekly Book Review":

"This is in a class with the propaganda novels of Charles Reade or Harriet Beecher Stowe, which is a pretty good class to be in. The happiest fortune we can ask for it is that it may be read not by the completely tolerant members of our large populace but by those, so much more numerous, who either have not had occasion to face the problem it propounds or who choose simply to close their eyes to it. If it can help them, indeed, to focus on the ugly sight it discloses, self-interest as well as decency may well compel them to take some kind of remedial measures."

The *New Yorker* of that day, less interested in helping our large populace to focus on the ugly sight of anti-Semitism, laconically says: "A pertinent idea for satire these days, but enough is enough and you get the point long before Mr. Miller has finished belaboring it."

So there we have an aspect of the public-relations-versus-art dialogue.

And yet, when you think—1945—the death camps were being liberated.

Me in your skin, was what Arthur Miller wanted the great populace to think about. You in my skin. Anybody could be anybody. Let's realize that, and be kind. Because the next gentile or Jewish life you save could be your own.

I don't mean to make fun of this idea. I find it a noble and moving one. Empathy—responsiveness to lives other than one's own or one's family's or one's nation's—seems to me still to be one of the highest human attributes—and rarest.

The gentle, liberal views of Arthur Miller were not the ones generally expressed by Jewish writers. Miller has said somewhere that he vowed never to characterize his people as Jews because he did not want the bad traits he might write about to be added to the burden of calumny Jews already had to bear in the world.

On the contrary, most Jewish writers couldn't wait to add to the calumny.

In justice to their rage, it must be said that they had their reasons.

The scene was the suburban Jew, the fat cat in postwar prosperity, very much at home out of Zion, having abandoned Jewish learning for himself and his children; or else keeping it somewhere in a side pocket, where it would not interfere with money-making American pursuits.

It was a scene ripe for the satirist. The Patimkins of Philip Roth's "Goodbye Columbus" leap to mind.

Since there wasn't much in the present scene that called forth the Jewish writer's sympathy (Malamud mostly had to reach back to earlier times and types to express his pity) the satirist's tone took over. It was an age of satire anyway.

Jewish writers really let post-war prosperous Americans have it. However, since the Americans they knew best were often Jews, they portrayed their Americans as Jews. A harmless transformation, but deadly in its way. It came to seem to many readers that the faults of Americans or human beings in general were exclusively the faults of Jews. From faults in the sense of flaws to faults in the sense of "things caused by" is another easy transformation, and deadly.

I think again of Arthur Miller's idea of never making a character Jewish. Ought we to be skeptical of that reasoning? Was it really a way of responding to the lure of universalism?

An experience-hungry book and literary landmark was Bellow's *The Adventures of Augie March,* published in the early fifties. Much admired, envied, and imitated. Life is an open class-room. A smart Jewish boy can liberate himself.

More than a decade later, Portnoy's complaint seemed largely to be that he was not Augie. "Because of you, my American-Jewish family," Portnoy was complaining, "I can't let myself go with the gentile *or* the Jewish hedonists. I can be bad but I can't enjoy it."

Who isn't angry at being cheated?

Why not be furious if your craving for hedonism is inhibited by only secular tatters of Jewish ideas?

Even out of great ignorance, it was still possible for a "Jewish writer" to write a "Jewish book" merely because of living in New York, or Cleveland, or similar places.

One had inherited, literarily speaking, a trust fund. Without even trying, one had certain speech rhythms in one's head—colloquialisms that were inherently funny, relationships always good for a cutting down by wit, and a large, energy-radiating store of culture-abrasions.

In *Joy to Levine!*, my first novel, I used some of the elements that were at hand. Levine has an overprotective father, who fears for his son's luck out in the world. And so Levine concocts an elaborate lying pattern with which to keep his father misinformed, and this makes up the main mode of the narrative. Levine falls in love with a girl who he thinks is not Jewish, and is delighted and appalled at his own adventurousness. Levine's friend is an Irish pro-Semite who uses Jewish comedy-routine speech patterns.

Although I had only the vaguest understanding of an aspect of Jewish life that, so far as I was concerned, had never made it to American shores—I mean the great ethical concepts embodied in Jewish thought—nevertheless, I looked about me and I wrote what was called a "Jewish" novel. And apparently I did not write so badly. I was praised for what I wrote, and so were many other Jewish authors who wrote as I did, with the eyes alone. What we saw and noted in our books still reverberated, luckily for us. We were drawing interest on money that an earlier time had put into our cultural bank.

In this wide-open meadow of sitting ducks that the Jews of America had become for the Jewish novelist out gunning for them there was only one impassable place. And that was the Holocaust.

The Holocaust is the central occurrence of the twentieth century. It is the central human occurrence. It cannot therefore be more so for Jews and Jewish writers. But it ought, at least, to be that.

Yet by and large, American Jewish writers have omitted it from their work. Not only have they not treated it directly (and there are authentic reasons for not doing this), but also they have not in most cases allowed it to color their response to Jews.

I cannot rid myself of the nagging thought that the experience of the Holocaust ought to have acted upon Jewish writers in the way we know that the encounter with devout Polish Jews acted upon the Russian writer Isaac Babel, who had wished to be assimilated into the Red Cavalry, the Cossacks; and upon the young German intellectual, Franz Rosenzweig, who saw them praying on Yom Kippur, just before he was to effect his conversion to Christianity. Both men, through these encounters, became Jews—Rosenzweig a learned and devout one. In short, the encounter changed their lives.

Let us suppose that the Holocaust did have this effect upon Jewish writers. I think, in fact, that it did. That it shook their souls with pity, with awe, with empathy and identification, and with the desire to know what it was that had been lost.

But how was the Holocaust to be written about? How could the virtues of fiction—indirection, irony, ambivalence—be used to make art out of this unspeakable occurrence?

To make bad art would be unforgivable. Even to make good art would be in another way unforgivable. Because that would be a transcendence. And it was not yet the right time for transcendence—it was far too soon, and maybe it would never be time.

If something is unspeakable, then how speak of it? Unless it is a metaphorical unspeakableness. But nothing about the Holocaust was metaphorical.

Years later, the Vietnam War was said to be unspeakable. Yet the Vietnam War was spoken about every moment of its existence, and TV cameras were always upon it.

Not so the Holocaust, which occurred in the deepest silence of the truly abandoned.

If something is unspeakable, then how speak of it? Is there a difference between writing and speaking? Yes, writing is more silent. Heart speaks to heart in the novel. It is inherent in the very

start, it meant she would never marry or have children. She meets her counterpart in the next generation—a young woman who learns of the evil and touches it through watching the Eichmann trial on television. This woman is pregnant. And obsessed by the fear of what is passed on in the cycles of human generations.

I decided that neither of these women in the book was to be Jewish. Clearly, a Jew might respond this way. Non-Jews *ought* to respond in the same way, I thought, and in my book at least, they would.

Heart's Witness, I wanted to call the book at one time. Anyone in America who *knew* and who *felt* was also a survivor.

My theme was what might happen to people who truly took into consciousness the fact of the Holocaust. I was not considering the meaning of the Holocaust for Jewish history. I was considering the meaning to human life and aspiration of the knowledge that human beings—in great numbers—could do what had been done.

I added to the characterizations:

I made my protagonist, at the time of discovery, young—and vulnerable to horror. I made the moment of discovery the precise moment of sexual seduction, almost of intercourse itself, so that everything should be open and the appearance of penetration complete.

In addition to the reasons I have already given, I also made her not Jewish so that there should be no historical inuring to the idea of mass torment of Jews in history, no stoical endurance, no religious apologetics. The catastrophe of knowledge was total.

When a child is born to the second young woman, it is the blood and guts of childbirth itself that brings the horror home to her.

For it's not only love that pitches its tent in the place of excrement. But all our human effort rises from that stage also. And if the pitiable human frame is humiliated, not cared for, mocked in its helplessness, then all sinks quickly down, down into ooze.

It was not that I wished to say that hospitals—or labor rooms in particular—were like concentration camps. I was not talking about the banality of evil. But rather that this small experience of seeing how easily the helpless are despised brings home—again, to the body as well as to the mind of the second woman—this knowledge that brings with it a limit to hope. She becomes, in her hallucination, the women who gave birth in the camps. It is the "taking in" of the knowledge of the Holocaust.

I had read documents: the Black Book of Poland and the diary of Emmanuel Ringelblum; I had myself been a daily listener to the testimony of eye-witnesses at the Eichmann trial.

After I completed the book I began to read what I had not read before. André Schwarz-Bart's *The Last of the Just.* The non-Jews who wrote about the Holocaust and who were mostly Germans, the so-called Group 47, with their own reasons for their own obsession with the subject, a need to explore the German psyche. Günther Grass evoked in his novels a surreal landscape, a deformed and grotesque cast of characters to suggest corruption at the marrow. Jacov Lind wrote of near-insane characters, bizarre transformations of the flesh. Kafka again, but now after the fact. Lind called one of his books *Landscape in Concrete.* Peter Weiss appeared to write from Marxist impulses; and Hochhuth, in *The Deputy,* documented what everyone suspected all along—that the silence of the church was deliberate—that Christianity's hostility toward Jews kept it quiet at a time when keeping quiet meant Jews would die.

It was Kafka who said that a book should be an axe to break up the frozen seas within us.

I felt, of course, when the book was finished, that I had failed to make a sharp enough axe of the book, had failed to live up to that material. Nothing can live up to that material but the Black Book of Poland, the journals of Emmanuel Ringelblum, the eye-witness who spoke at the trial of Eichmann of Jerusalem, the poems of the children of Teresienstadt.

But I was not prepared for the book to be praised for showing the corruption of evil in everyday life—unfaithful husbands, corrupt landlords, ill-run hospitals, etc. That is, when it was praised. When it was not being taken to task for being too dark a book, or one in which the effect is "to isolate the narrator," as one reviewer said, "from what we like to think of as the real world. . . ."

The question the book was asking—What kind of daily lives can people live after they have touched an evil so absolute that it overpowers all the old ideas of evil and good?—eluded some reviewers entirely.

Nor was I prepared for a review which regretted that I had left out something. *"Touching Evil,"* the reviewer said, *"lacks the comedy of Mrs. Rosen's Green and Joy to Levine! (Perhaps, to be taken most seriously, a writer must first make us laugh*—a paradox that Mrs. Rosen wrung out of her earlier books.)"

I hope no one will mind my adding italics. It's the only way I have of showing now how despairing I felt to read that mindless line. What did the reviewer want from me: a song and dance about the Holocaust?

I've since come to think there might be some truth, at least in the first part. Out of sheer despair over the tone of Jewish humorists (they were never in any review characterized as merely funny—the obligatory word was always "wildly" funny, an attribute originating, I have the impression, with Dorothy Parker in *Esquire,* and thenceforth never relinquished by her or anyone else), it may be that in reaction I plunged the book into the darkest tones I could summon.

No one can think of the Holocaust without thinking of the image of the Jew in the world, and particularly in literature—most particularly in the literature created by Jews.

This brings me now to the second part, the wisp of the tail. And that concerns writing itself.

I'll start off with a small anecdote.

Recently the editor of an old and well respected magazine told me that he was giving a lot of thought to a literary form he had just invented, but not yet got onto paper. He called it, in his own mind, the new fiction, rather than the now-familiar new journalism.

What he had in mind was to assign certain topics to serious fiction writers and tell them to go ahead and treat the topics in the writer's own characteristic way.

Thus the reading public would get insight, through the techniques of fiction which alone can move us (unlike the essay, which only makes us think) into the personalities and news of the day. The editor didn't want us all to have to wait—and this is crucial—until some particular writer came along with that particular donnée. That might be too long to wait. That might be never.

For a moment, when he suggested it, I was intrigued. After all, every writer knows how sometimes the unsought task set by the story itself brings forth an aspect of response the writer didn't know about before and is pleased to have been able to uncover.

And every writer has had the experience of finding that at some point the story may call for the appearance of a particular character about whom nothing is known, yet who must, with the greatest dread and fear of failure, be invented, based on nothing. And sometimes it happens that out of nothing, something comes. The character based on nothing is invented on the spot, and is more vivid than the one for whom the story exists.

But then I thought about what this really meant: that this one aspect of fiction writing, the donnée, or what is given—which has always been considered to be the one mysterious and almost mystical, certainly incontrovertible fact about writing, that a certain writer at a certain time feels an irresistible desire to write about one particular thing in a particular way—would be taken away from the writer.

Henry James said it was as useless to quarrel with a writer about the donnée as to quarrel with a man about the color of his eyes.

This sacred-to-writers-accident of the donnée was to be taken away. In its place, the assigned topic.

The editor is not a bad man. Not a philistine, not a fascist. In fact he's a good man, with deep concerns about the issues of the day: and a sensitive man, with a love of poetry and art. A man, in fact, who himself once was involved in the writing of fiction, but who gave it up for a long and successful career in journalism.

Here, maybe, is a clue to what launched the editor on his invention. Journalism, with its assigned topics, its pre-set length, its clear-cut form and its admirable correlations of assignment to result, makes him—makes many of us—impatient with fiction, which blunders, which meanders, which waits for its donnée in order to begin at all and then, often, fails, in the working out, to achieve the full reach of possibilities of its own idea.

Why, I asked myself, couldn't Jewish writers assign themselves the task of repairing the damaged image of the Jew, and also make it art?

And then I answered myself: because art comes from sources that are beyond the reach of the rational, that are not wholly within our control. A writer who functions as an artist and not as a propagandist cannot be sure that what is written will brighten up anybody's image in the eyes of the world.

The dilemma is that fiction, literary art, cannot deal directly with ideas without ruining itself as art.

Good fiction searches for itself in the same way that truth does. By utter freshness of response. This means respects cannot be paid to pieties that have been emptied of meaning for the writer. The problem of anti-Semitic fiction written by Jews will not be easily solved. There is always the ferocity of attention to those near at hand.

Our decades have nearly forgotten how to make heroes and heroines out of people of virtue. Writers have forgotten how to write about them, and readers have forgotten how to be attentive to them.

And yet—and yet. There was one day, in the depths of the Israeli-Arab impasse in the desert, when the Egyptian Third Army was encircled by Israeli armor, when the Israelis were holding their position as leverage in bargaining for the return of their prisoners, and when the Egyptians exerted their leverage of cutting the nations off from their supply of oil, and when there had begun to be a series of pieces appearing on the OP ED page of the *New York Times*—one day by an Arab, the next day by a Jew, as if by such evenhandedness someone had planned to cancel each by the other, ad infinitum—one day there appeared a piece by Freidrich Duerrenmatt.

It was a short statement to announce that he aligned himself with the Israelis. "For all of us," he said, "so we won't soon all be silent."

Impossible to read that without remembering Duerrenmatt's play, "The Visit," in which a whole town is bought into collusion against a single man, bought pair of feet by pair of feet by the bribe of new shoes. And I thought again how it's not enough for us to know the facts. Not enough to have the documents, the history, the accounts in the daily papers, the pictures on the eleven o'clock news. Because we do not recognize our lives until we read them in art. We need that shock of recognition.

The world won't be changed by it—we ought not to expect that. All that will happen is that we will be brought up abreast of our own lives, whose meaning and weight cannot crush what they illuminate.

To write as a Jew in America, it is no longer enough to draw on the interest of what was put in the bank long ago by others. It means somehow to find ways of being "interesting, highly interesting," to quote Saul Bellow again, while yet not, as he warned we must not do, substituting public relations for truth or for art.

When Flannery O'Connor was asked why Southern writers wrote about freaks she replied, "It is because we are still able to recognize one." In order to have that recognition, she said, "You have to have some conception of the whole man."

The central struggle of O'Connor's stories appears to be to drag, assault, mug her characters to the same perception.

Debased Jews in American novels are not reminded—neither roughly nor gently—that they have fallen from a kingdom of priests, a conception of the whole man. Does the author even think of it?

If what the writer is really writing about is debased Americans, why make them Jews? But if the writer is writing about Jews who don't recognize their grotesqueness, why shouldn't they be brought face to face with it? Why else the piled-up faggots and the roaring fire? What other conversion—if the writer keeps the claim to prophet—can the roasting be for?

If writers are going to put on the prophet's mantle let it not be half a mantle but a full one. This means that they must educate themselves to the point where they will never again be able to see the distortions of Jewish life in America without also seeing the vision of what ought to be.

Exactly how might this be done? Being a fiction writer, I can't give anyone, or myself, a blueprint. I would have to feel my way as I went. But there are two quotations from an essay by Franz Rosenzweig, "Towards a Renaissance of Jewish Learning," that might do for a start.

The first is: "Hebrew, knowing no word for 'reading' that does not mean 'learning' as well, has given this, the secret of all literature, away." And the second is: "Nothing Jewish is alien to me."

How else can we have a literature that will not shame us by proceeding as if the Holocaust had never been?

—1974

Simone Weil—A Dissenting View

Simone Weil had the kind of genius that marshals all fact, all history, all literature, all culture to one consuming interest. With her great learning, she strove to connect fragments of Pythagorean geometry, Jesus, Krishna, Plato, American Indian tales (the marriage of Dirty-Boy and the daughter of the chief becomes the Incarnation and the Redemption), Gilgamesh and Sanskrit, the Cather and Manichean heresies, Chinese Taoist writings and universal folklore. All of them, she said, led to "the truth."

The poor chaplain of the Free French Forces who came to see her complained: "What confusion . . . the acrobatics of a squirrel in a revolving cage! . . . it would be a hundred times better to be a peasant with no more culture than a good country priest. . . ."

Her notebooks are filled with this ceaseless connecting. "Flight of Christ into Egypt. The hidden infancy of Dionysus, or Orestes. . . ." "Non-Euclidean geometry. Parallel lines meet if one regards the infinite as finite. Orders of infinity. Cantor." In the mysterious poetry of impacted thought, connections leap up faster than words can catch them. Here is a passage that might fit into a page of Virginia Woolf's Journal: "Waves. Whole and parts—Same and Other—Horizon in midocean. We are encircled by our own vision. Pan, god of shepherds. Shepherds at Christmas. Vocation of labourers: the contemplation of things."

We see her in our mind's eye—dressed in her dark, serviceable cape, her beret squashed down on her short black electric hair, her round, child-sized spectacles barely covering her large inquisitive eyes. She is hurrying off to teach her classes, or to demonstrate, or to talk in union-halls to the workers, or to sit through all-night sessions with her cotheorists of French radical politics of the twenties and thirties. She rushes breathlessly and awkwardly, sometimes impatiently and self-destructively. At the Spanish Front she rushed into a pan of boiling oil. Because of the dreadful injury she had to be removed for treatment, much to the relief, we gather, of comrades who worried about the zeal (despite her pacifism) with which she handled the gun she didn't know how to shoot.

She was astonishing in her capacity to see how things connect and just as astonishing in her capacity for blindly not seeing—and no one could argue her out of either position.

In all ways but one, the biography of Simone Weil by her long-time friend and fellow philosophy-student, Simone Pétrement,* confirms beliefs about Weil already held by readers—the brilliant mind, the passion for justice, the obsession with the Catholic Church, which she could neither embrace whole-heartedly nor leave alone. But the biography also suggests another area that stuns. Simone Weil was implacably anti-Semitic. Religious meditator that she was, she gave to her bigotry an elaborately theological basis.

The question then arises that is at the heart of all morality. Is it possible to be regarded by history as brilliant, high-minded, pure-souled . . . and also be a bigot? Is bigotry only idiosyncrasy, like left- or right-handedness, for which we make allowances when encountering the otherwise noble mind? Or is it the worm that creeps into the soul and corrupts all doctrine?

The appearance of a detailed biography makes it possible to ask the question in more specific form. Can Simone Weil, who was an anti-Semite, also be what almost every one of the friends referred to in this biography calls her—a "saint"? Or is there in anti-Semitism a willful ignorance that must corrode the anti-Semite's philosophy even while it maintains the anti-Semite comfortably in prejudice? Easy to prove, among the stupid, the resounding yes to this question. How is it possible in the case of Simone Weil? Her biographer, untroubled by the moral question, reverently prefaces with one of her own: "There are few men or women who would not feel unworthy to touch such a life. So the question must be asked: Who am I that I dare to speak out?"

Weil died in 1943 at the age of 34, of self-starvation. Ostensibly this was done in sympathy with the deprived French workers, but whatever the real reason, certainly it was out of deep division

---

Simone Weil, a Life, Pantheon, 1978.

within her soul. Dare I jog her now on her bed of pain? I cannot do otherwise. Her frail and brilliant life holds all the keys to the great moral question confronted here.

It is possible to put bare bones together in such a way that the skeleton of Weil's life begs for beatification. Here are the bare bones. She was born into an assimilated Jewish Parisian family of considerable culture and education. She was attracted to Catholicism, but refrained from baptism (because of certain scruples). She studied with the famous activist-philosopher, Alain, at the Henri IV Lycée, and later, after she received her degree from the École Normale, she was sent to the provinces to teach philosophy. She waived the privileges of her advanced degree and accepted no more pay than the lowliest of school teachers. She was throughout this time reading, writing, organizing demonstrations on behalf of the workers, with whose lot she thoroughly identified. She was linguist, philosopher, philologist, mathematician, scholar of ancient civilizations. But in order to feel more keenly the suffering of the workers, she tried dangerous factory work, then heavy farm labor, always at the risk of her already frail health. The works that grew out of these experiences, *Waiting for God, The Need for Roots, Gravity and Grace,* and countless essays on political issues of the day all reflect her compassion for the suffering of the oppressed. Throughout her life, and despite persistent and savage migraine headaches, she deprived herself of all material comforts for the sake of this identification. Having fled with her parents to America to escape the oncoming Nazis, she contrived to get back to England where she wrote and planned with her friends for the resistance of the Free French Forces, contracted tuberculosis and died of starvation caused by her efforts to limit her nourishment to something less than what a French worker would eat during the German occupation.

Since her death, these bones have been regarded with veneration. The effect of the biography, one critic complained, "is to obscure and blur by detail." Indeed, the fleshing out of the life, though done with continued reverence by the biographer, gives us deeply disturbing vignettes—so many that only a few can be referred to here.

Throughout her life, Weil could not bear the physical touch of friends or family. On one occasion she deliberately burned a deep wound in the back of her hand with a cigarette. She wore shoes that opened sores on her feet and in every way possible contributed to her own physical debility. She refused to eat enough to keep her healthy, she sought out freezing hovels to live in, and often had to be rescued by her well-to-do parents, particularly by her mother, who would toil up the stairs to her tenement apartment and secretly plant small sums of money there which Simone, always contemptuous of ledger-keeping, would delightedly discover and spend.

Her behavior toward others was often characterized by what one of her correspondents charged her with—"moral indelicacy." For example, the workers complained that she injured their self-regard because she addressed them as "wretched." They did not think they were. She scandalized the peasants with whom she lived for a time by never washing her hands before the milking, out of her own stubborn notion (a false one) that the peasants wouldn't either. She caused deep pain to the wives of the workers when she stayed up with their husbands to debate union matters. They were blindly jealous of these all-night brainstorming sessions and she once without explanation strong-armed the wife of a friend who momentarily stood in her path. The biographer tells us she may have expected to have this woman bar her way through the door as the wives of workers often did.

Finally, she who looked about all her life for ways to inflict suffering on herself, who could so easily have fulfilled her goal of martyrdom by calling herself a Jew in German-occupied France, refused to acknowledge herself as one. She left religion out of the questionnaires, not as civil libertarian, but because she fell short of baptism and because Catholicism was for her the only Christianity. Dying in a sanitarium in England, she refused to respond to a nurse's practical inquiries about religion, but divulged her dilemma at length when the doctor came round. If it seemed possible to inject a note of humor into her life—it doesn't—we might hear an echo of Woody Allen's quip about identity: Jewish, with an explanation.

All her life, this dilemma swirled about her and her Catholic friends and the priests to whom they sent her. Was she ready for baptism, or wasn't she? The greatest stumbling block to her conversion was her unwillingness to accept Christian acceptance of

Judaic roots, the connection between what she referred to as the Hebrew God and the Christian God. "At the center of all her oppositions was her attitude to Israel [the people, not the nation], it was the key to all her resistance," wrote one of the priests who questioned her. When the Vichy Government deprived her of her teaching post, she suspected it might be because of her Jewish origins. Her letter to the Minister of Public Education must be one of the most loathsome examples of intellectual detachment on record:

> I do not know the definition of the word Jew; this subject has never been part of my program of studies. . . . Does this word designate a religion? I have never entered a synagogue and I have never witnessed a Jewish ceremony. . . . Does this word designate a race? I have no reason to suppose that I have any sort of tie . . . with the people who lived in Palestine two thousand years ago. . . .

As usual, her biographer pads after her. Simone, she says, was trying "only to demonstrate the difficulty of defining the word 'Jew.' "

When the invasion of France by Hitler seemed a possibility she wrote, incredibly: "No doubt the superiority of the German armed forces would lead France to adopt certain laws of exclusion, chiefly against Communists and Jews—which is, in my eyes and probably in the eyes of the majority of Frenchmen, nearly an indifferent matter in itself. One can quite well conceive that nothing essential would be affected."

Could she have spoken with such cruelty of the fate of the Jews if she had not been born a Jew? Was it because of her own desire for humiliation, torture, martyrdom that she felt "nothing essential would be affected"? Did she make the profound spiritual error of not granting separate identity to those who resembled her, transgressing fearfully in that case against her own idea of "attention," the respect due another human being?

What upset her most bitterly about the biblical Hebrews and their "so-called religion" was mainly and obsessively the account of the destruction, commanded by God, of the Amalekites in Canaan. The monk Vidal, after exhaustive talks, complained that Weil "would not admit one could explain these things . . . by the harshness of customs in that period, or by the necessity to preserve the Jews from any contact that could have altered the purity of their monotheistic faith." He found her clearly "not for baptism." She meditates upon the heavenly warning to the Hebrews against contamination by the Canaanite practice of child sacrifice, and cannot accept common biblical and historical exegesis, because it favors the Hebrews. "'Making your children pass through the fire,'" she muses in her New York notebook. "It cannot be a sacrifice, because it would amount to a massacre. It must refer to a form of baptism."

J. M. Cameron (in *The New York Review of Books*), comments on a puzzle: Weil "seems insensitive to the ethical content of the Torah and doesn't come to see, as she might very well have done had she devoted as much time to the study of the Old Testament as she did to the writings of the Greeks, that the moral ideas of Christianity, above all the two great commandments of the Law, love of God and love of neighbor, come from the Torah. Simone Weil was so wonderfully intelligent that there is a puzzle here." He then suggests that the difficulty may have been her training, "the great French discipline, *explication de texte*," which leaves out commentaries of historical study and the light that shines from context. But at once he adds, "In justice to her . . . she had a marvelous sense of historical development."

So lack of history is not the answer to the puzzle! What is, then? It's tempting to say, "the anxiety of influence," the literary theory put forward by Harold Bloom to explain how it is that creative people can go on creating even though they know their predecessors have probably said it all: they deliberately but of course unconsciously "misread" their predecessors in order to give them flaws they didn't possess. In this way they free themselves from the achievements of the past, so as to be able to create their own works. Kept to the realm of poetry, this is innocent enough and damages no one. Translated to theology, the way leads to the inquisitorial fires.

Or, to have another go at explanation, here are George Eliot's words in the mouth of Daniel Deronda: "Some minds naturally rebel against whatever they were brought up in, and like the opposite; they see the fault in what is nearest to them."

The final explanation may elude us, but not the fact—which is that Weil's adulthood encompassed the years of Hitler's power, and that she heaped vilification on the Jews at a time when millions of them were dying. They were to her an "accursed people," she records among similar jottings in her 1942 New York notebook.

T. S. Eliot, in his 1952 preface to *The Need for Roots,* said, "She was . . . suffering torments in the affliction of the Jews in Germany; yet she castigated Israel . . . " (in the sense of the people). Eliot does not give us his source for the first part of the sentence. There is not one jot written down about that. However, it's possible he heard her speak words to that effect. Just as one day she said to her friend, Dr. Bercher, "Personally, I am an anti-Semite," she might on another day have also said, "I am suffering torments about the destruction of the Jews." But the record shows nothing of that.

All of her life was one long meditation upon subjects dear to her thinking. Little by little she came, because of the force of that thinking, to reverse her ideas on certain matters. She was first an ardent pacifist who applauded appeasement of Hitler. After the fall of France, she wrote: "My criminal error . . . concerning pacifist circles and their activity, was due to incapacity caused by the devastation of physical pain for so many years. . . . I failed to detect their propensity for treason." Always an activist on behalf of the workers, she came to believe that revolution was not possible "because the revolutionary leaders are ineffective dolts. And it is not desirable because they are traitors. Too stupid to win a victory, and if they did win, they would oppress again, as in Russia. . . ." She had been a staunch antinationalist (some of her hatred of Jews stemmed from their longing for a national homeland). But when France signed the armistice with Hitler, Weil, appalled, joined the Free French Forces. (She badgered everyone with a plan for front-line nurses of which she would be one. They would be gloriously killed, she explained, but no matter). In an English sanitarium, suffering from a mild case of tuberculosis, she raged against her comrades who kept her from the underground resistance in France, and wrote military recommendations meant for de Gaulle. What else might she have revised her thinking on? Suddenly it was too late. She refused to take nourishment—literally ate herself alive ("More than anything else, I fear remorse," she had said).

All her life she had sought martyrdom, yet she understood that a looked-for martyrdom was useless and inauthentic. In her New

York notebook, the following prayer is written: "That I may be unable to will any bodily movement, or even any attempt at movement, like a total paralytic. That I may be incapable of receiving any sensation, like someone who is completely blind, deaf and deprived of all the senses. That I may be unable to make the slightest connection between two thoughts, even the simplest. . . . May all this be stripped away from me, devoured by God, transformed into Christ's substance, and given for food to afflicted men whose body and soul lack every kind of nourishment. And let me be a paralytic—blind, deaf, witless and utterly decrepit."

What terrible irony there is in this search for martyrdom in the context of the death of six million Jews about whose fate, at the hands of the Germans, she had said "nothing essential would be affected."

The discovery of exclusion of a whole people from a mind that has been cherished for its generosity and compassion is scalding knowledge. What? No room for me and mine in a system so large and gracious? The anger I feel is undercut by the piercing sadness of Weil's life. Could she not foresee that all her works would come to nothing? Why did her ignorance continue? In my confusion I create a fantasy experience for her like that of Franz Rosenzweig, another assimilated Jew who yearned for Christianity. On what was almost the eve of his conversion, wishing to enter Christianity through Judaism as the first Christians had done, not "through paganism," he attended Yom Kippur services with an elderly Polish Orthodox congregation. Thereafter he wrote that conversion "no longer seems necessary to me and . . . no longer possible" and became a devout Jew. In my fantasy, Weil did not have to go so far. Only to see what Rosenzweig had seen. About the Jew on the Day of Atonement, Rosenzweig wrote: "He confronts the eyes of his judge in utter loneliness as if he were dead in the midst of life . . . God lifts up his countenance to this united and lonely pleading . . . in this moment he (the Jew) is as close to God . . . as it is ever accorded man to be."

Here I am stymied. I think this must be the fault of the Jews. Simone could not be wooed by the beauty and mystery of Kol Nidre night. Because of "he," not "he and she." If Weil, like Rosenzweig, had wanted to enter Christianity through Judaism and had visited a synagogue, where was the room full of devoutly praying women with whom she could feel identified? Was it then this piece of stupidity, which has kept women from the synagogue because there is no central place for them, that had also kept Simone from sympathetic seeing? But this turns out to be a false trail. She had no qualms about the masculine bias of synagogue or church. She had no wish to enter Christianity through Judaism. And her only visit to a synagogue in her lifetime was during her New York year, for which occasion she hunted up what must surely have been alienation's diadem: a black synagogue in Harlem.

And so there is nothing to stop her headlong rush into meaninglessness. To anyone whose consciousness is raised to the truth about the fate of Jews in those years every pious, unselfish, self-sacrificing, "saintly" utterance of Simone Weil's falls into ashes. "Compassion is what spans this abyss which creation has opened between God and the creature," she wrote in her notebooks. But about the Jews herded into ghettos, she continued to be, Pétrement tells us, "severe": "I would much more prefer to go to jail than to a ghetto." As if she'd been asked to make the choice!

In *The New York Times* of January 23, 1976, Elizabeth Hardwick remarks that she preferred the Simone who predated this biography. "From the incomplete translation of her work and from the dramatically reduced and vivid moments of her thought and life, she . . . (had) taken on the clarity of the very reduction itself. The life was as if given in panels of stained glass, each frame underlined by a quotation from her writings and quite unlike any others of our time." Now, however, this biography has "obscured the life with details."

What the details are, we have seen. And now, I believe, the process has inexorably reversed itself. When one of those unforgettably beautiful quotations is heard—for example, out of the factory: "The affliction of others entered into my flesh and my soul," and, "The feeling of personal dignity is shattered. One must forge another kind," we will not be able to stop ourselves from thinking of the life and its context—Europe in the late thirties and early forties. It will not be possible to avoid knowing, at the same instant, what those terms, "dignity" and "affliction," meant in the death camps. And then we will remember that among the quotations there is not one that refers to them, or that speaks with compassion of Jews. And it will be as if Simone Weil, who set herself the task of a lifelong meditation upon human injustice, had devoted her time to traffic violations, while all around her the air rang with cries of murder.

—1978

The Bird Has No Wings:
Letters of Peter Schwiefert

In 1938, Peter Schwiefert, a half-Jew, fled Nazi Germany to live as a self-declared Jewish refugee—first in Portugal, where he was imprisoned, then in Athens, where he was penniless. Peter's father, a playwright, and his stepfather, a member of an influential Prussian family, were gentiles. Peter's Jewish mother passed for German. All were furious at him for leaving. Under their protection, they said, he could have weathered the bad times in Germany. His declaration of being a Jew was to them an act of willfulness.

"I've never seen such a handsome men," one of Peter Schwiefert's friends had said of him. "Everybody loves you," was engraved on a gold chain given to him by a girl at the age of 19. But at 21 he was a refugee and began his outpouring of letters. These letters* should be added to the dark treasure of Holocaust documents. They are the testament of one who began as the Jew Hitler made and who ended as one who chose to be a Jew.

We fill in for ourselves the replies that are not there. A Holocaust world rises from fragments about people and events. The father, for example, goes on writing plays under Hitler, the stepfather divorces Peter's mother and takes an Aryan wife, the Jewish grandfather dies alone, the Jewish grandmother is taken to a camp and gassed.

Most of the letters were written to the mother Peter Schwiefert adored. He played down the hardships he suffered. He asked for news of her safety and the safety of his half-sisters, who did not even know they were Jewish, and of his Jewish grandparents. But mainly he begged his mother to be brave, to join him in exile, to save his grandmother—not to abandon her or let her be taken

---

*St. Martin's Press, 1976.

away. Above all, he wanted her to acknowledge in her heart that she was a Jew.

His mother responded (we fill in) by promising to come to him but never coming, by inviting him to visit her in her faked Aryan existence in Bulgaria and then withdrawing the invitation, by declaring to him her dislike of Jews, by converting to Christianity in a sudden effusion of religious feeling at the very time Peter was writing her of his exaltation at declaring himself a Jew.

Part of a family that lived on self-delusion and lies, Peter alone equated truth with sanity. He longed to make an authentic self even in the madhouse. He wanted also to be a writer, but there was no time—"the bird has no wings."

Is there anything in these letters to show the writer he might have become? Two things: he used writing as a tool for thinking, and he uttered the true cry of the writer who is faced with something to be done: "I have forgotten how to write!" Meaning that in writing there is no memory of how the thing was done before; each thing is new, and must be invented. Who but a writer would think to utter such a lament?

If we compare the voice of these letters to that of another young and cut-off Jewish writer, Anne Frank, we must also look at the circumstances of each. Anne Frank wrote her diary within the security of her family. The hiding place is still a recognizable world in miniature. The diary is so full of charm and wit that it has become one of the Holocaust documents that postwar Germany has been able to take to its heart. The deepest horrors of her ordeal did not begin until after the diary ended, when she was taken to a concentration camp. Then there was no more family, and no diary.

Peter Schwiefert's letters are written from a world in which the heart has already been torn out. He is alone and terrified for everyone he loves. He is without support, except for the wavering help of Jewish agencies, which often themselves were sinking under the load of victims they sought to help, and who hardly knew what to make of this volunteer refugee and half-Jew.

Anne Frank ended her diary: "I still believe that people are really good at heart." Peter Schwiefert's last letter to his mother, written in 1944, says this: "And you see, Mother, what they've done to our own people, to all the Jews who hadn't a chance to get away—what they've done to them in the Polish camps and in the ghettos! . . . Who is responsible? The nation, of course, which gives itself such leaders, perfect representatives of the general vileness, and which chooses them because it recognized itself in them.

"Yes, they have all recognized themselves: the killers, the assassins of Lublin and the gas chambers, the thousands of killers who coldly shot, mowed down, gassed, buried alive, burnt alive; the populace who followed or preceded the killers, the populace who broke windows, pillaged houses, ill-treated, humiliated, beat up; and then those who didn't know, who didn't want to know. . . . If Hitler had been dealing with honest men he would have remained what he was—a charlatan. But he knew who he was singing his dirty songs for, and we know too. . . . He touched them where they were evil and terrible, where his call awakened a thousand echoes. . . ."

After three years, as a refugee, Peter was able to join the Free French Forces. "What we live for, what we believe in—beauty, art, dignity, freedom—will be restored to us," he wrote. He asked for permission to be circumcised but was refused, discovered his love for Jerusalem, which he visited on leaves from the Syrian campaign, and was killed two kilometers from the German front only months before the end of the war. Among his possessions were two Jewish prayer books and a silver Star of David.

Included at the end of the book are a few letters from some of the personae of the drama. Peter's mother, sick and bitter, returns to Germany after the war and judges herself (even as she tries to convince herself that her mother may have died a natural death). She writes to Peter's father:

"I've been a bad daughter just as I've been a bad wife and a bad mother. . . . Have I ever really achieved anything at all? Hasn't everything been silliness, frivolity, levity, thirst for pleasure, erotic delight, selfishness? Do you see your faults as clearly as I see mine, and do they torture you? Mine torture me."

Her judgment does not seem too harsh. And yet, at times it looks as if it may have been Peter Schwiefert's Proustian love for his mother ("Oh, please do come soon. . . ." "My longing to see you is indescribable. . . ." "I don't love you only as a mother, but also as a woman, there's no other word. . . .") that gave him hope and joy in exile, that kept him warm until he died.

So again, within the ghastly numbing horror of this not-yet-forty-year-old story of how six million Jews came to be killed, there leaps up the complicated and infinitely moving tragedy of one— and of one by one.

The book's editor, Claude Lanzmann, has shown his belief in the force of these letters (until now in the possession of Peter's surviving half-sister) by reserving most of his biographical comments for the latter part of the book, and allowing the letters to speak first for themselves. The collection was published initially in France, and the translation is double—German into French (except for the handful of letters written in French) and then into English (except for the few in Peter's own excellent English). But as far as I can judge, the mind and heart are revealed intact.

—1976

Bernard Malamud and the Accidents of Influence

"As a writer," Bernard Malamud said in an interview in the seventies, "I've been influenced by Hawthorne, James, Mark Twain, Hemingway, more than I have been by Sholom Aleichem and I. L. Peretz." More recently, Malamud mentioned Michael Seide as an influence. I eagerly tracked down Seide's short-story collection *The Common Thread*, published in 1945, and found a sensibility and an interest in word play closer to Henry Roth's than Malamud's. Whatever sparked between the two writers remains mysterious and personal. Unless it was simply that Malamud, having steeped himself in American "great writers," came upon Seide's work in the forties, saw there someone shaping Jewish material into art and thought, "Why not I?" Since this conjecture reflects something of my own experience, the reader is free to regard it as intrusively subjective or happily intuitive.

In the late 1950s I attended as student a writers' conference in Colorado, bringing with me a short story later published under the title "The Open Window," about a family whose daughter struggled for autonomy with, I hoped, more comedy than pain. The father and mother, closer to my grandparents than to my own parents, spoke in the rhythms of Jewish Brooklyn. A then known critic at the conference told me he liked my work but for "obvious reasons" couldn't judge it: "Find a Jewish writer or critic to show it to." The year was 1958. I lay on my bed in Colorado feeling lonely for New York and finding it hard to breathe in the pure air of that altitude. A copy of Malamud's *The Assistant* had come into my hands and I read it through instead of going to classes. Its impact was like a clap of thunder from one of those Colorado mountain peaks. In my innocent joy I cried out to the bare room: "I understand how he did that!"

ably to one survivor of it: "The German Refugee." I had a chance to note it again in the recently published collection of Malamud's selected stories.*

This sole story Malamud wrote on the subject is about a German Jew who has escaped Hitler and come to America, but lost everything in the process—work, language, gentile wife. He is offered a chance to establish himself in this country by delivering a lecture in his field at a place resembling the New School. But for that he must curb the heavy accent that makes his speech all but incomprehensible, master his terror of speaking in a foreign tongue, and—what radically inhibits his progress with his American tutor—overcome the hopelessness that paralyzes his will. Refugee and tutor meet in one agonizing session after another, but the refugee can only rail against the betrayals of ex-country and ex-wife, whom he calls anti-Semite. At the eleventh hour the fog lifts, the refugee is able to rouse himself to master what must be mastered, and he delivers his speech brilliantly. But when the tutor next comes to visit, he finds the refugee has put his head in the oven. The tutor then reads the refugee's mail: a letter from Germany tells that his non-Jewish wife, having converted in his absence, has been taken away with other Jews and killed.

I asked myself why I forgot that story at the time. Rereading it now, I think I must have felt that it was so removed from the tone and moral weight of everything I was then reading—the diaries of Emanuel Ringelblum, the testimony of the witnesses at the Eichmann Trial—that I had to forget it. "I suffer for you, you suffer for me," Morris Bober told his assistant. When that connection is broken, the Jew can only stick his head in the oven as the German refugee does, even if that is where others wished his head to be. The placement of moral weight still seems to me startling. The story makes the demand that the sufferer, the Jew, must ensure that suffering does not warp him and further separate him from others.

Somehow in those fifties stories about Jews debased by suffering—Susskind the schnorrer and thief in "The Last Mohican," the wife in "The Loan" who won't lend money to her husband's needy friend because her own losses frighten her too

---

*The Stories of Bernard Malamud, Plume, 1984.

much—the importance of lashing Jews with their own experience to make them remember why they are in the world works. But can the experience of a just-barely escaped Holocaust survivor be subsumed in the mythos of Malamud's gentle Depression sufferers, who never had any greater worry than having to sit in the dark to save on the gas bill? Can direct experience of the Holocaust be made into a symbolic journey about how to live life more humanly? When the surreal effect of reality exceeds anything to be derived from mythos or symbolic heightening, can it be forced into the lines of a morality tale? I disagreed so greatly with Malamud on this that apparently I had to forget about the existence of his tale.

Flannery O'Connor wrote story after story in which the moment of illumination—grace—precedes death by an instant, indeed is thrust upon the character by a death that advances as inexorably as a bull with lowered horns. Those stories have drawn a view of Christian life as mere tip-of-iceberg. The unseen part is what's important: afterlife—or whatever it is that follows the moment of enlightenment-in-death. O'Connor's stories are wonderful to read and to teach—their construction is so four-square, their subjects so riling. But the influence of O'Connor's stories on me has been to make me know that if I can be said to have a theology at all it is not O'Connor's. For Jewish writers (those, that is, who care about this sort of thing in the first place), illumination followed by death is no good. Jewish life, like Torah, is on earth. With the exception of "The German Refugee," the only Malamud story I can think of that ends in death, Malamud's characters are pierced by illumination in time for life on earth. (In "Take Pity," the death leads to someone else's illumination, another matter entirely.)

It is always necessary, when a writer has made a great impact, has invented a new voice and subject, to remind oneself of what things were like before he or she came on the scene. It is the achievement and tragedy of such a writer—it happened of course with Hemingway, with Faulkner, some have even claimed to see it happening with Bellow, with Singer—to appear in later works to be a self-parodist. We are taught something extraordinary by a new voice, but when we hear it again we ungratefully say, "I know that already! Why are you imitating some writer from the past whose name I've forgotten?"

For me the great contribution to be reminded of in Malamud's work is not magic, angels, or demons, delightful as they may be: it is the work of repair. As in Kabbalistic Judaism, the theme of Malamud's fiction has been nothing less than restoration of the fallen world, sometimes through deeds, often through individual spiritual transcendence whose impetus springs from some startling source. What is not-I teaches me what I am. Sometimes the not-I is what might be called a "rogue" Jew, sometimes not a Jew at all. In "The Last Mohican," it is thieving Susskind who brutally teaches Fidelman how to give up everything in order to begin to understand anything at all. In "The Lady of the Lake" the Jew who denies he is a Jew in order to win a woman who poses as a gentile aristocrat discovers she is a Jew who cannot accept anyone so ready to deny his birthright. His false name, Freeman, becomes a mockery of his condition as too late he proclaims that he is bound to covenant. Though peripherally a Holocaust story—Isabella del Dongo reveals at its close that she bears a Buchenwald tattoo on her breast—the pitch of the narrative places it more truly among secular tales in which an elusive stranger leads the way to redemption (in this case, a failed one). Kessler, in "The Mourners," is put out of his mean top-floor room by Gruber the Jewish landlord. Each has crippled his life with selfishness: Kessler has abandoned a family (having denied life, he earns his meager living as an egg-candler by peering into life's mysterious beginnings, looking for flaws) and become a bitter recluse; Gruber, obsessed with property and greed, has developed a heart condition. Neither Jew feels pity for the other. When snow falls on the dispossessed Kessler and his few sticks of furniture out in the street, it is the old Italian woman who begins to shriek at the sight of him and doesn't stop shrieking until her sons carry Kessler and his belongings back up the stairs, break the padlock on the door and install him in his room. Only after that does the landlord come upon the egg-candler sitting in mourning—"How, in so short a life could a man do so much wrong?"—and join him: "With a cry of shame he tore the sheet off Kessler's bed, and wrapping it around his bulk, sank heavily to the floor and became a mourner." One could go on. In *A New Life* it is through Pauline Gilly that Levin can finally embark on the hard road toward becoming a mensch, when he takes on the impossible burdens of her broken marriage.

What a treasure to come upon for a writer struggling with the shards of her own perceptions, the fragmented portions of Jewish life to which she was born! And I can see what it would mean to the Southerner to come upon Eudora Welty, the Midwesterner upon Sherwood Anderson, the Catholic upon O'Connor or J. F. Powers, the black about-to-be writer upon Ralph Ellison or Zora Neale Hurston; can see what those efforts of imagination and sympathy could offer by way of take-your-breath-away, experience-opening influence that show where one's own writing in America might tend.

Malamud has revealed that when he married a non-Jew his father "went into mourning" for him. Those elements are elegantly transmuted in "The Magic Barrel" when Stella, the fallen woman who stands in red shoes under the lamplight, is wooed by Leo Finkle, the rabbinical student. Around the corner Stella's father, the tricky marriage broker who has cursed Stella and pronounced her dead, says kaddish. We who are accustomed to think "prayer for the dead" should remind ourselves of the contents of that prayer: nothing but praise for the redemptive powers of God.

Does Malamud have writer-followers? Although I once believed myself one, I now have to say that I don't think so. Who could duplicate such idiosyncratic intensity? Maybe Malamud wanted every story he wrote to say something to his father about who he thinks is a real Jew, despite intermarriage or nonobservance. That leaves the rest of us creating images in books in the best way we can, having started with the recognition, foolish perhaps but with generative power, that hidden in someone else's perfected art is the homely thing one knows. Influence is no more accident than the lung's extraction of oxygen from elements of air. The soul's definition is what influence becomes when it teaches us to know about ourselves what we had no way of knowing we already knew. To paraphrase Morris Bober, "I write for you, you write for me."

Homage is due to Bernard Malamud. Though he reaches easily and well for the comic touch, he has shown that it is possible even in a long career, and in a context largely of satirical American writing, never to fire off in a single story a cheap or reductive shot at Jews.

—1984

The Literature of Contempt

More than ten years ago, when I was teaching a fiction writing seminar at the University of Pennsylvania, I learned that my office was the one Philip Roth used when he taught there. My desk, I became acutely aware, was his desk—and in a drawer was a newspaper clipping with a photograph of Roth, though I myself may have put it there. It was a stern portrait, Roth's dark brows drawn together in a frown, which reminded me of a scowling portrait I had seen of Flaubert.

Portnoy's Complaint had recently been published. I was tempted to print beneath the photograph "*Mme. Portnoy, c'est moi,*" and leave photo and caption there for the model to meditate on. For a couple of years, I regretted that I hadn't done so. I thought: if Roth could see, as Flaubert had seen, that the character of the woman in his book related more closely to himself than to a sociological portrayal—in Roth's case to a kind of final word on the destructive Jewish mother—there would be some justice in that.

One hesitates to say too much for fear of bringing another muscle spasm on Nathan Zuckerman, that good writer. Or, what would be even worse, on Philip Roth, an even better one.

But it's impossible to avoid noting that over the years Roth seems to have become caught in a Jewish writer's nightmare. He is the Jewish writer so stuck in subjectivity that he can't get out, forced to write about material he clearly hates. He is the child who will not be weaned, who clings to the breast long after the mother is desperate to get away. Jewishness is his breast, yet there's no nourishment in it for him. He is too old, and the breast of his choice is too empty; he only mauls it with his teeth.

Even though I didn't print "*Mme. Portnoy, c'est moi*" beneath Philip Roth's photograph, I feel now that Roth has done it for me. He has become Mme. Portnoy, the nag, the screamer. And as he locks his teeth around her nipple, which has become his own nipple, he seems like a figure out of Dante's *Inferno*. ("What was your crime, poor unfortunate?" "I made a breast that was limp and slack, and had no milk in it, and I said it was Jewish society.")

In those years, I felt angry at Roth's work and the work of other Jewish satirists. For me the central question was—and is still— how to write as a Jew after the Holocaust. How to write as a Jew and as an artist, with honorable effort toward both those attributes.

Not to say, "I am a writer who happens to be a Jew," as if that happening were of no greater significance than an event in Central Park. Of course one "happens" to be a Jew—one happens to be everything one happens to be—and everything one happens to be digs into the soul.

In the course of trying to analyze what it meant to me to write as a post-Holocaust Jew in America, I once wrote an essay, "The Holocaust and the American-Jewish Novelist," in which I looked at some of the ways the Jew had been treated by Jewish writers. I was dismayed that the Holocaust had made so little difference to many Jewish writers, who still regarded Jews as fair game to be satirized because they were fat cats and/or ignorant vulgarians. Jewish mothers were smothering; Jewish daughters were princesses; Jewish sons were trying to get out from under all that and touch America, because of course they were the ones who would become the writers.

It struck me that something was wrong, and that whatever this was could not always fit into the easy formulation that pits the integrity of the artist against the Philistine. Or against the wish of the rank and file of Jews for the "sentimentalizing and sweetening," as Saul Bellow called it, of Jewish life.

The trouble seemed to be closer to the warning sounded by Delmore Schwartz in his short story, "America, America:"

> The lower middle-class of the generation of Shenandoah's parents had engendered perversions of its own nature, children full of contempt for everything important to their parents. Shenandoah had thought of this gulf and perversion before, and he had shrugged away his unease by assuring himself that this separation had nothing to do with the important thing, which was the work itself. But now as he listened, as he felt uneasy and

sought to dismiss his emotion, he began to feel that he was wrong to suppose that the separation, the contempt and the gulf had nothing to do with his work; perhaps, on the contrary, it was the center; or perhaps it was the starting-point and compelled the innermost motion of the work to be flight, or criticism, or denial, or rejection.

For years, the Jewish writers most likely to be mentioned at the Modern Language Association panels on Jewish American writers were those in the triumvirate who protested they weren't.

Bellow, the philosopher-poet, generally avoids satire, and prefers to bathe his subjects in an affectionate poetry. (Except when he writes about women; then he switches to naturalism.)

The stories and novels in which Bernard Malamud engages most Jewishly are set in earlier times, as if he sees Jews best in the past—preferably the Depression past—where he can pity them.

Roth, the writer whose prose has the most topspin to it, is the satirist of present-day society. Of the three, Roth appears to have the most imitators and followers.

It's not difficult to see why this is so. Roth is, of course, supremely talented, but lesser writers reading him can get the idea that it is possible to write about Jews with the eyes and ears alone—that you don't have to know much more than what you see and hear. A writer living in a big city like New York, or Newark, or Cleveland, where there are plenty of Jews, could keep his or her eyes and ears open in the family and on the buses and pick up the prose rhythms that are so helpful in enlivening the pages of books.

Such a writer might have been writing about the most personal or private aberration, but the prose rhythms were there and thus another Jewish novel was born.

Ten years after that early essay of mine, I am still brooding about what—if anything—is wrong with men and women writing the most negative images into their books, if that is how they see the Jewish world. Nobody wants censorship or outsiders dictating what writers write. And it isn't that I see Jewish life so differently from the way those writers do.

If we write about the nobility of Jewish thought without mentioning the vulgarity and the debasement of Jewish life, we are sentimentalizers. But if we write about debasement and vulgarity without showing or knowing that there has been a defection from the nobility of Jewish ideas—what shall we call ourselves?

After the publication of Hannah Arendt's book, *Eichmann in Jerusalem,* in which she criticized the Judenrat, the Jewish council appointed by the Nazis to enforce their anti-Jewish decrees, Gershom Scholem wrote to her to say that she lacked *"ahavat Yisrael"*—love of the Jewish people.

Scholem didn't mean that Arendt should have suppressed information about the behavior of the Judenrat, but that she ought to have included other information as well, or other attitudes, that would have shown her understanding of their desperate situation.

Could such a standard ever be adopted by fiction writers? Certainly it would be a startling idea for many, and might even repel some. Modern literary modes are more geared to attack than defense. Modern writers can tolerate being regarded as distanced, detached, alienated, affectless, chilling—anything that suggests higher intellect—but dare not risk empathy for fear of being labeled apologists.

To have "ahavat Yisrael" needn't make the writer an apologist. But it might add a deepening tension to what the writer makes of the chaos of American Jewish life.

In today's American publishing world, the genres most encouraged in Jewish writing seem to be Jewish satire and Jewish scandal. Nothing in such a market encourages the Jewish writer to teach himself or herself Jewish texts. As a result, this chaos of Jewish life for most Jewish writers—with a few notable exceptions—is without a context of Jewish ethics or morality or vision. Jewish life, for these writers, has no truth other than the possibly debased form in which it comes to them via family connections.

In the past, serious non-Jewish writers have occasionally felt a certain responsibility to create Jews of virtue—in some cases, to counteract bad images of their own creation. George Eliot in *Daniel Deronda* created idealistic Jews as well as materialistic ones, and Charles Dickens tried to balance Fagin by very different Jewish characterizations in later books.

But most serious Jewish writers do not reflect that responsibility. I get the feeling that Shakespeare had more compassion for Shylock than some Jewish writers for their characters.

A recent novel by a European-born Israeli reinforces a point about patterns of American writing. Aharon Applefeld's *Baden-heim 1939* was read by many with a sense of astonishment. Could this be a picture of Jews about to go to the gas chambers—these selfish, self-deluding pastry-eaters?

Applefeld himself supplies a clue to the answer. In an auto-biographical essay, he tells us how he escaped the Nazis and lived in the forests for three years. Before the Hitler era, his parents had elected to hide their Jewishness. "Don't sound like a Jew," they told him. In the forests, he is *forced* to hide his Jewishness—but he discovers there that the one thing that gives him inner distinction, the thing he can cling to and that helps to sustain him and save his life, is what he calls the "sweet secret" of his Jewishness.

One understands, then, his fury at parents who sought to rob him of the very thing that gave his life meaning in the face of death. But if he clones his parents a hundred times in one novel, do we then have a picture of Jewish-German society under Hitler, or of hated parents cloned a hundred times?

Do I have a formulation for what Jewish writing ought to be? If I had such a formulation, such a cause, it would be the weakest cause there is—an appeal to the personal responsibility of the writer to live more fully in the tension between, on the one hand, the need to shake off, throw over, murder, those deficient Jewish mothers and fathers, and, on the other hand, to respond to the appeal of these mothers and fathers for the only redemption there can be for them—justice in Jewish books. The critic Harold Bloom wrote in "Jewish Culture and Jewish Memory" that modern Jewish intellectuals are more influenced by Freud, Kafka, and Gershom Scholem than by Akiva, the second-century Talmudist, and for all I know he is right. But it seems to me that many Jewish fiction writers—even if they don't know it, and never heard of him—are paying homage in their writerly hearts to Akiva.

How else explain the rage they express at their misguided as-similationist families who kept the sweet secret of Jewishness from them? Or their disgust with members of the Jewish middle class who abandon Jewish idealism for materialism, or for self-serving, self-protective Jewish clannishness?

It is as if even those Jewish writers who have least connection with the Jewish culture of the past were lamenting, reviling, castigating in the voices not of Freud, Kafka, and Gershom Scholem, but of prophets—though they may be prophets almost wholly ignorant of their own texts and contexts.

For there is no literature I know of to compare with it, nothing like American Jewish literature for seething rage at its own subject and subjects, nothing like the spectacle of Jewish writers who have looked about them at Jewish life and in response have produced the literature of contempt that in 1940 Delmore Schwartz warned us would be coming.

—1984

The Second Life of Holocaust Imagery

Recently an eminent Jewish historian claimed that what readers of Holocaust literature want is not more documentation, but someone to infuse meaning into the terrible facts. What readers want, the historian said, is novelists.

Jewish tradition has always been more than text; it has also been the experience of text. Not only what occurred or was said, but how it is interpreted—commentary. When the tradition was whole, said the historian, Yosef Yerushalmi, there were mystics and great poets to give it meaning. Now we must turn elsewhere.

A call to the imagination of a people to repair the work of reality—to recreate a destroyed world by infusing meaning into the very events that destroyed it—what else could be more moving? Yet also alarming. Elie Wiesel, yes; André Schwarz-Bart, yes; Nelly Sachs, yes. These Europeans possess a tradition of grandeur in language and idea. But the American-Jewish novelist has not by and large been concerned with grandeur. Comedy, satire, one-line jokes—these have been what the American reading public most prizes in the Jewish novelist. Thinking of American fiction writers as a whole, we may be tempted to say, Alas for meaning. With such meaning-bestowers, who needs nihilists?

If novels are to be, as Yerushalmi indicates, a reflective source of something like a wholeness still hidden from us, clues buried somewhere in the creative imagination, whose creative imagination will they come from?

The energy that sprang from the immigrant generation's break from ghetto life created a fervent literature celebrating freedom and—from the very beginning—mourning the loss of connectedness. It gave birth to a fireworks display of novels and poems, from bittersweet American success stories like *The Rise of David Levinsky* to countless poems of sharp disappointment in the new world.

After that, though no doubt sociologists were writing about how safe, how prosperous, how educated and well integrated Jews in America were becoming, for the novelist there came loss after loss, observed and commented on: the corruptings of assimilation. Jews became materialists in the way they viewed their Jewishness—which was, beneath the comedy, the terrible message of those Jews in Philip Roth's "Eli the Fanatic," who feel threatened in their Waspy suburb by the arrival of a tiny Hasidic remnant from Europe.

Dr. Braun, the narrator of Saul Bellow's novella, "The Old System," remembers the anguish of the old Jewish family feuds. "A crude circus of feelings," he calls them. "Oh, these Jews—these Jews!" he exclaims to himself. "Their feelings, their hearts!" What, he wonders, was all this emotion good for? "This old-time fervor?" The implication is that perhaps what it was good for was the old time religious passion. With that gone, only grotesqueries, passions without real goals, are left.

In *Zakhor,** a slim book of enormous reach, Yerushalmi tells us that when Jewish belief dies Jewish history is born. For many Jewish novelists, the Jewish component is no longer a matter of struggle, tension, dialogue, or dialectic. All that is over, and can be portrayed, if at all, as belonging entirely to the past.

The choice for reader and writer lies between two approaches: on the one hand, railing hotly (even in the shadow of the Holocaust) against a maddeningly less-than-perfect Jewish presence; on the other, relegating that presence to the past, embalming it as something sweetly nostalgic and then dismissing it and burying it with the dead. The tension of such a choice echoes the dichotomous nature of the identification dilemma posited for our post-Holocaust time by two Jewish philosophers.

Emil L. Fackenheim argues that surviving Jews present a posthumous victory to Hitler when they fail to live as conscious Jews. Michael Wyschogrod replies that the real victory to Hitler is coercion of any kind. Reinstate choice—including choice to decide *against* being a Jew—and you wrest ultimate victory from the would-be defeater of the Jews. (With such victories, Jewish irony is sure to comment, who needs defeats?)

---

*The Jewish Publication Society of America, 1982.

But the greatest paradox forms about the Holocaust, it seems to me, for novelists, in the tension between writing and not writing about it. If the writer treats the subject, the risk is that it may be falsified, trivialized. Even a "successful" treatment of the subject risks an aestheticizing or a false ordering of it, since whatever is expressed in art conveys the impression that it, too, is subject to the laws of composition. Yet not to write means omitting the central event of the twentieth century.

For years writers who cared anything about the subject at all have been saying that the Holocaust must not be reduced to art, must not become metaphor. Too great an enormity for art, containing it in some form conveys the message that the Holocaust is no longer the hellish explosion of demonic forces it was: it can be controlled, organized, disciplined like any other difficult subject. Elie Wiesel, among others, has spoken of the agony of creating within this tension.

Holocaust imagery has often been widely misused, from casual reference on the one hand to S&M pornography on the other. But there is a way, I believe, in which the Holocaust can legitimately infuse life.

The Italian writer and Nobel prize winner, Eugenio Montale, speaks in his essay, "The Second Life of Art," of the way in which certain images from literature reverberate for him at intense moments:

> I cannot see a line of . . . mourners at a funeral . . . without thinking of Italo Svevo's *Zeno;* or look at certain modern *merveilleuses* without thinking of Modigliani or Matisse; I cannot contemplate certain caretaker's or beggar's children without having the Jewish baby of Medardo Rosso take shape in my mind; and I cannot think of certain strange animals but the zoo of Paul Klee opens in me. . . .*

We cannot see a full grown retarded man without thinking of Faulkner's Benjy in *The Sound and the Fury;* cannot see a poor storekeeper staying open long empty hours without remembering Malamud's Morris Bober in *The Assistant;* cannot see an intelligent and idealistic young woman badly matched in her mate

---

*Eugenio Montale, *The Second Life of Art*, ed. and trans. by Jonathan Galassi (New York: Ecco Press, 1982), p. 22.

without thinking of Dorothea Brooke in George Eliot's *Mid-dlemarch*.

To those who might argue that such a response is merely a kind of "literariness," a tic found among people incapable of response except through the medium of someone else's words, one can only reply that for better or worse print has been imprinted in us. In those eras and among those people where Bible stories sank in deep enough, all life was experienced through their prism. That is the point: we are an analogy-making species, with minds that learn via connections. There lies our hope and also our danger. *What* we connect and *how* we connect it are vital keys to our understanding and can be discussed and at times corrected. *That* we connect is a given.

Examples of what shapes perception need not be limited to art. Certain penetrating images that come from knowledge of the Holocaust may do the same.

One of our human goals, we are frequently reminded, is to try to understand the suffering of others. Sympathized with, yes, but can someone else's suffering be felt? The answer is obvious. Another's suffering can be understood and felt only through one's own suffering. But what if one's own suffering, terrible as it is, does not approach the sufferings of another? Then the law of human communication is unchanged. We must still work from what we know and try to connect it to what we do not.

Novelists, too, are notorious connectors. They make meaning by linking one thing unexpectedly to another. Connecting means broadening and that, in the case of Holocaust suffering, comes dangerously close to universalizing away the particularity of the experience. When done best, what is broadened is also deepened in communicating power. At its worst, broadening can turn the deepest experiences shallow.

"Only *don't* connect," E. M. Forster might also have significantly said, since we fail so often in our comparing and contrasting.

A drop of self-reference now will tint these waters no matter how carefully I try to keep the tube capped. Some recent books on Holocaust literature that discuss my novel, *Touching Evil*, published in the late sixties and recently reissued, maintain that the novel universalizes Holocaust images. Because my feelings at the time of writing the book were certainly not universalist but rather terribly and painfully particular, fixated, obsessed with the fate of Jews, I feel a strong need to examine the concepts that lie behind such readings. Is it possible I could so have betrayed my own heart and mind as to have done what these critics say I did? Or is there something else to consider here, namely, a misunderstanding of the attributes of specificity and a misnaming of universalism?

Touching Evil deals with the response of those not involved directly with the Holocaust except through imagination, and examines its impact on them. I chose non-Jews to do the responding in order to extend as far as possible the reach of the Holocaust upon these "witnesses-through-the-imagination." I made this self-imposed rule: one was not to invent new Holocaust happenings— *that* would somehow be adding to the sum of pain. Not to say one was there if one was not there, not to invent that cheap bravery. But one could write about response here, being heart's witness here. (Others have disagreed with me and have written honorably from within their views.)

In *Touching Evil,* two women have been stricken by knowledge of the Holocaust: one through watching the Eichmann trial, televised daily in the early sixties; the other through reading documents and seeing photographs of the death camps.

Universalism implies a weakening of the specific Jewish experience by broadening it to include what all people experience of suffering. If a novel says, as *Touching Evil* does, that the Holocaust experience is so intense that it radiates out to affect non-Jews who then experience it through the imagination, then that is not universalizing, not a generalizing, a spreading and thinning-out of the Jewish trauma, it is the opposite: a bringing of the non-Jew into Jewish experience. It is not universalizing; it is Judaizing.

In the novel a woman gives birth. She has watched, all during the latter months of her pregnancy, every day of the Eichmann trial, with its eyewitness accounts of atrocities—the first full, continuous account of them the world had known. This is her *Shoah,* that runs not for nine-and-a-half hours but for months. In the hospital labor-room she is flooded with remembered images. Above all, of the woman who gave birth in lice-infested straw, watched by a booted guard who held a torch "to see how life begins," and who then flung the newborn to the crematorium fires. Bodily pain awakens in her a sensory knowledge of that other woman's pain. It is not the same, of course—her baby will survive; she will be cared for in the hospital. But the moment of bodily empathy is there, an imperfect kind of understanding to be sure, but a kind of Holocaust understanding all the same. A woman protected in America, and non-Jewish, has been possessed by knowledge of the Holocaust. This, I believe, is not diminishing the Holocaust to universal experience; it is imprinting certain universal experiences with the pain of the Holocaust, Judaizing artifacts and events.

Trains and toilets, labor pains and hunger. For a mind engraved with the Holocaust, gas is always *that* gas. Shower means their shower. Ovens are those ovens. A train is a freight car crammed with suffocating children: it arrives at the suburban station in a burst of power and noise, there is a moment of hideous hallucination that is really only remembering, and then one steps into the train and opens the newspaper. Of course this does not always happen. Some days the sky is simply blue and we do not wonder how a blue sky looked to those on their way to the crematoria.

But when it does come, this unwilled re-experiencing, this "second life," must not be turned away from, imperfect though it may be. We hold on to the images of the Holocaust, guarding them jealously, as we must, against misuse by writers. We criticize Sylvia Plath for comparing her father to a Nazi, herself in her inward agony to a Jew, in her poem, "Daddy." We cringe or glare in anger when someone mindlessly compares a subway crush to a cattle car on the way to a concentration camp. Yet such images continue to come unbidden to the mind. When the mind is more sophisticated, it remembers to add: "If it is like this for me here, what must it have been like for them there . . . ?" Reaching for similes is an endless human endeavor. We stretch the little we know into the vaster unknown. Understanding that we do so is our sanity, and making distinctions between what we know and do not (or cannot) know is our moral intelligence.

There is an irony in my reference to Montale. In one of Montale's poems, "The Prisoner's Dream," the prisoner of tyranny speaks in this manner: "The purge never ends, no reason given." *

---

*Trans. by William Arrowsmith in Eugenio Montale, *The Storm and Other Things* (New York: W. W. Norton, 1985).

Next comes a passage meant to create a transition from pain and degradation to beauty and joy: "I've looked around, conjured up / rainbows on horizons of spiderwebs, / petals on the trellis of my bars. . . ." But then a shocking image: "I've sniffed on the wind the burnt fragrance / of sweet rolls from the ovens. . . ."

Two words: "burnt," and "ovens," as in crematoria.

Perhaps not everyone, but surely no prisoner of tyranny, and no writer about such matters, should register those images without despair. (Bernard Malamud ends "The Loan," a story that takes place in a baker's shop and speaks of the Holocaust, with the same images: "She . . . with a cry wrenched open the oven door. . . . The loaves in the trays were blackened bricks—charred corpses.") And so when Montale offers them in a context of transcendence and hope, the poem flies apart. Montale, from whose literary concept I draw support for this idea of a second life of Holocaust images, fails us in this instance. In the poet's desperate pursuit of wholesome associations, he appears to have suppressed Holocaust-consciousness.

For the past extracts a debt from us. We are not permitted the use of certain words or associations without giving them their due, and their due is what devolves upon them from their original context.

In the universal experience of a woman in labor (even though in a modern hospital, even though her child will be safely delivered) there reverberates, for those who remember it, the agony of the woman who testified at the Eichmann Trial. This double rite of passage—particular to universal and universal back to particular—is all we have to keep us humanly connected. Otherwise we fall victim to a pathology of Holocaust hoarding, a refusal to let its images embark, as they must, on their second life.

I agree that for Jews universalism is something to fear. But that fear ought not to force us into misreadings that stifle and stunt possibilities open to Jewish writers. A thinning-out of Holocaust images in such a way that they diminish the force or meaning or memory of their origins would be unforgivable. But entering into a state of being that for whatever reasons makes porous those membranes through which empathy passes, or deep memory with its peculiar "thereness," so that we can move, as far as it is given to us to do so, into the pain and hence the meaning of the Holocaust— that, too, is a kind of memorial.

Surely the novels of Elie Wiesel, and most especially the memoir, *Night,* have been read by fathers and sons all over the world. In the radical relationship of that doomed time, in which everything is stripped away from parental and filial feeling except the obsessive wish to keep one another alive, along with the guilty desire to go on living at any cost oneself, may we not guess that whole generations of fathers and sons see the mirroring of themselves?

One day, perhaps, a young woman nursing her baby in her own safe house, who has read Cynthia Ozick's "The Shawl," will feel the pain of that mother's sight of her starved infant in a way that is immediate and profound. Or she will experience in her love for her own child the magnitude of the mother's loss in Susan Fromberg Schaeffer's *Anya.* Via an osmosis of empathy, though she and her child are protected and healthy in America, she will infuse her own experience with the terror those stories convey, a second life of art. And since that art is a Holocaust re-creation, the woman's response will be a Holocaust memory of a sort, and we must let it be.

And then perhaps a novelist will write of that woman's experience. And so connectedness and continuity evolve. The manner of it may disturb us with its impurity, but in the end this may be the deepest kind of ongoing Holocaust memorial that we can have.

—1987

On T. S. Eliot:
Geniuses and Anti-Semites

How are we to think about them, our literary geniuses and intellectuals who are anti-Semites—casual or rabid, now-and-then, or through and through? The poet W. H. Auden proposed one point of view:

> Time . . .
> Worships language and forgives
> Everyone by whom it lives;
> Pardons cowardice, conceits
> Lays its honours at their feet.
> Time that with this strange excuse
> Pardoned Kipling and his views,
> And will pardon Paul Claudel,*
> Pardons him for writing well.

Apparently time has pardoned T. S. Eliot, too, for writing and publishing directly anti-Semitic lines in his poems, and for calling in his prose for the establishment of a culture from which Jews would effectively be excluded. This year is an Eliot Centennial. Though the *New York Times* reported that some English Jews were balking at contributing sums to a celebration, other English Jews were heading up the fundraising.

In America, the celebration booms ahead *fortissimo*. Eliot's poems have been treated to marathon public readings by prominent literary figures in every available public space from university halls to rentable theaters. Prompted by the publication of Volume Two of Eliot's biography by Lyndall Gordon, *Eliot's New Life*,** and the first volume of Eliot's letters,*** retrospective apprecia-

---

*Claudel's plays were performed by the Nazis in Vichy France.
**Farrar, Straus & Giroux.
****The Letters of T.S. Eliot*. Edited by Valerie Eliot. Volume 1. 1898–1922. Harcourt Brace Jovanovich.

tions of the Eliot *oeuvre* have appeared in major journals, most
without reference to the offending lines in the poems or the
slanders, direct and implied, in his prose works. Taken altogether
they are not many but they are prime.

"Burbank with a Baedeker: Bleistein with a Cigar" opens with
reference to antique grandeurs, "the God Hercules," and
Cleopatra, whose "shuttered barge / Burned on the water all the
day." The poet brings us to modern-day Venice:

> But this or such was Bleistein's way:
> A saggy bending of the knees
> And elbows, with the palms turned out,
> Chicago Semite Viennese.

> ***

> The rats are underneath the piles.
> The jew is underneath the lot.
> Money in furs. . . .

At its close, the poem asks:

> . . . Who clipped the lion's wings
> And flea'd his rump and pared his claws?

The voice (in parody, of course, since it is Eliot) is the voice of
Blake, inquiring of the Tiger, burning bright: "What immortal
hand or eye, / Dare frame thy fearful symmetry?" Blake's implied
answer is praise of God's creation; Eliot's question can be answered only by a curse. Eliot's culprit is rat-like Bleistein, who
gnaws at culture's underpinnings, lower-case Jew that he is, responsible all by himself for the fall of civilization.

In "Sweeney Among the Nightingales":

> Rachel née Rabinovitch
> Tears at the grapes with murderous paws . . .

In "Gerontion":

> My house is a decayed house,
> And the jew squats on the window sill, the owner,
> Spawned in some estaminet of Antwerp,
> Blistered in Brussels, patched and peeled in London.

As if to civilize Eliot's anti-Semitism, his biographer points out
that it was occasioned not merely by personal revulsion against the

mercantile, lower-case (in Eliot's poem) Jew; Eliot was after nothing less than a reconstitution of a Christian civilization.

These thoughts are developed in *The Idea of a Christian Society*. Here Eliot cited as his aim the "creation of a temper of mind in people" that will enable them to recognize what is "*morally* wrong—and . . . *why* it is wrong.*"* Though this book, published in 1940, nowhere slanders Jews, it nowhere mentions them, either as contributors to, or victims of, modern society. The poet who regarded a great many fellow human beings with contempt and disgust (of these, Jews and women were foremost), sought to recover "the sense of religious fear, so that it may be overcome by religious hope."

When Eliot wrote in 1948 in *Notes Towards the Definition of Culture,* "The Western World has its unity in . . . the ancient civilizations of Greece, Rome and Israel," it is clear, in the light of the earlier work, that he meant Israel via its transmutation into Christianity. *After Strange Gods,* the book of a decade earlier, had spelled out Eliot's program to eliminate Jews from the intellectual community. Writing about how to develop a tradition anew, he said, "What is still more important is unity of religious background; and reasons of race and religion combine to make any large number of free-thinking Jews undesireable."

When directly asked to comment on Eliot's anti-Semitism, American Jewish literary critics tend to dismiss the charges. Alfred Kazin quipped in the *New York Times* that if great writers were to be discounted because of anti-Semitism, there'd be nothing left to read. Irving Howe said staunchly that Eliot's anti-Semitism was the social, not the killing kind, and anyway he repudiated it later. But there is no trace of such repudiation either in the Gordon biography or the earlier Peter Ackroyd biography of Eliot, or in the recently published Eliot letters, or in the prose works published in Eliot's lifetime. While Eliot did later repudiate anti-Semitism in a private letter sent in the 1950s, it was not his own but the institutional kind, practiced by nations, that he meant. Of that, more later.

Clearly, objecting to the anti-Semitism of T. S. Eliot is, among Jewish intellectuals, the height of naiveté. "What about Dostoyevski, Dickens, Shakespeare, and practically everybody else?" is the countering question. "Western literature is riddled with anti-

Semitism." All true. Jews have been among the prime shapers of Western civilization, which has, in turn, responded by shaping their image with vitriol.

The knowing response of Jewish intellectuals to this matter sounds like some not-so-amusing inversion of Woody Allen's comic restaurant complaint: the food's terrible and besides the portions are too small. This time the food is a known poison, but because the portions are enormous (all those writers who were anti-Semites), we're supposed to swallow them down. As Jews we have in fact swallowed them down, as has Western civilization. What follows here may be regarded as an attempt to construct a receptacle into which a few pips may be spat.

Unlike Dostoyevski and Dickens and Shakespeare, T. S. Eliot, God-seeker and anti-Semite, is of our own time, an acknowledged shaper of modernism. Whether to contribute money for his centennial celebration or to drum it out of others seems a less central question than how we are to regard his art.

To give language and shape, as Eliot did, to what some consider the malaise of our time, cloaked in fastidious language and a poet's music, is no mean feat. Eliot's subject—exhaustion of feeling, lament for a vanished aristocracy of mind, hatred of the common clay—expressed, as he himself admitted, private emotional lack. By one of life's literary ironies, his personal wasteland vision came to seem the stance of an age. And by an even greater irony, that bleak vision continues to shape the view of the world of newer generations, allowing easy slippage into a pre-fashioned nihilism— what Saul Bellow calls "unearned despair." By the time Eliot's vision brightened in old age, it was because he was, with a new marriage, at last personally happy—but by then he had outlived his poetic talent.

That form and content are inseparable, that thought and feeling should be one, is one of our great modernist precepts. Eliot himself stressed its primacy in his essay, "The Metaphysical Poets," lamenting that when "the sentimental age began . . . poets . . . thought and felt by fits, unbalanced. . . ." When we praise Eliot's poems and hold, with the critics, that their anti-Semitic content is not worth noting; or when we deplore the content but praise the sensibility, we honor a poet whose content must be severed from form, whose feeling is unsubjected to thought.

An Oxford professor quoted in the *New York Times* argues for Eliot by saying that these poems appeared in the twenties and thirties; Eliot could not have foreseen the Holocaust. Apart from the fact that Eliot republished the poems after the Holocaust, the notion requires us to agree that these sentiments are not in themselves degraded or dangerous. They might have gone on whistling cheerfully through literary history, if only the Holocaust hadn't come along.

What is literature for?

On the simplest and most benign level it can show us how we live by reflecting our lives back at us, giving pleasure and a community of ideas and language. On the most exalted level it can become what Kafka said it should be: "An ice-axe to break the sea frozen inside us."

Jean-Paul Sartre, in *What Is Literature?* (1948), marked out the territory in this way: "No one could suppose for an instant that it would be possible to write a good novel in praise of anti-Semitism." Maybe we should take Sartre literally—"novel," not poem. Truth-in-fiction is a powerful force, a greater tester in its psychological stresses than poetry, which may rest on rhetoric to resolve internal questions. A novel is like a giant Calder mobile, all parts moving one against another; a miscalculation in the weight or force of one part will bring about breakdown of the whole. Certain works may wring from us a shocked attention to what is released from moral constraint: they have the feel of bold risk, but they cannot have moral grandeur.

Eliot aspired to a poetry of moral and spiritual grandeur. His *oeuvre*, pimpled with anti-Semitism in his poetic maturity, is now deeply scarred from that pox. His work will never afford a whole-skinned integrity, or the clear aspect of the highest art. Eliot never repudiated the anti-Semitism in his own work, or published an altered version of his view of Jews. He simply never publicly wrote of them again. But the published work of a writer knows no sequence: it is *oeuvre,* spoken of and taken as integrated whole.

I grew up on Eliot. When I was in graduate school in the heyday of New Criticism, no one offered apologies for Eliot's work: he was our modernist genius. Partaking of the general reverence, I read his poems, swallowed hard, and thought, "It's metaphor." I thought, like his present apologists, "He's only reflecting the culture." Now I think that poets have to do better than that. Especially if they are praised for being innovators. Especially if they set out to be modernists, who want to break with all the old trammels. "Make it new!" was Ezra Pound's cry. Eliot the innovator took it up. Between them they perpetuated the old and shameful slanders. Eliot was given the Nobel Prize; Pound, the out-and-out traitor who broadcast fascist propaganda from Italy during the war, received the Bollingen.

Documenting the failure of high culture in *Language and Silence,* George Steiner writes: "We know now that a man can read Goethe or Rilke in the evening, that he can play Bach and Schubert, and go to his day's work at Auschwitz in the morning." In that case, why do we still believe in literature, and want our children, students, and friends to love it? Despite Steiner's assertion that culture has failed, which I take seriously, we haven't many other choices. Maybe what we can still believe in is the capacity of literature to humanize and civilize those who are capable of it. It can't reclaim the world. Anne Frank, who at age thirteen believed that people were basically good, was murdered in Belsen at fifteen.

I have a friend who goes very far in her belief in the value of literary art. She gives it not only moral, but religious weight, insisting that the fineness of great art is one of the proofs of the existence of God. Where else can it originate, she asks—that rage for the perfection of form, for *le mot juste,* that Flaubert said he rolled on the floor to find while writing *Madame Bovary?* Now that heaven's the place bombs come from, says my friend, she thinks that the floor—the agonized effort of the artist to create something there— is not a bad place to look for a while. But what if we find there something as destructive of the spirit as bombs are of the flesh? Then it's time to rethink the question of whom and what we honor, and why. Little may alter, yet if consciousness is all, let us have all we can of it.

"The life of a man of genius, viewed in relation to his writing," Eliot wrote, "comes to take a pattern of inevitability, and even his disabilities will seem to have stood him in good stead."

Three women were in love with Eliot and he made use of their love, emotional support, and intellectual stimulation before he abandoned each in turn, with crushing results for them. His marriage to Vivienne, which provided a life of unalloyed horror for both parties, also provided inspiration for *The Wasteland*. When it was done, he signed her into a mental institution where she languished unvisited by him for the ten remaining years of her life. Her brother, a cosigner, visited her after a time and found her "as sane as myself"; Emily Hale, the childhood sweetheart who waited patiently throughout the terrible years of Eliot's marriage, found herself abandoned when Vivienne's death freed Eliot; and Mary Trevelyan, who believed herself to be the sole trustee of Eliot's love, was similarly dropped without a further word when Eliot wished to move on. For all these Gordon finds a pattern and tells us, "His passion for immortality was so commanding that it allowed him to reject each of these women with a firmness that shattered their lives."

Eliot is not the first literary man to count on women to be saintly or sacrificial. Henry James was another—though he repaid his debt to them rather better in literary portraits. It is touching to reflect that Eliot's doomed wife, Vivienne, at one point in her prolonged breakdown, saw herself as James's Daisy Miller, the madcap heroine who is misjudged by the puritanical and convention-bound Winterbourne.

Like many writers, Eliot presented several selves: the elegant publishing executive, the jokester poet-friend (with pet names for all—Eeldrop for himself and Appleplex for Pound), the severe church warden, the penitent God-seeker, the bawdy rhymester, etc. "Am I a humbug?" he asked Virginia Woolf in a letter. Woolf may have thought so. In her journal, she satirized him wearing a "four-piece suit."

The rosters of creativity are full of many-selved artists who evolved a single, stamped style in an attempt at self-integration. Eliot had his elegant perfection of clothes and manners, the mask-like demeanor. G. B. Shaw also cultivated elegance (concealment for the shaming past of an alcoholic father, early failures) along with an armor of brittle wit (Yeats dreamed of Shaw as a smiling sewing machine).

And there is a link to be found in the scandal of the recent uncovering of Paul de Man's early anti-Semitic writings, never revealed by him to colleagues at Yale. Some critics have found in de Man's deconstructionist literary theories an attempt at expiation. The argument, much simplified, goes something like this: The

anti-Semitic texts I wrote (and am concealing) were untrustwor-
thy; therefore I maintain that all texts are unstable. De Man, in
short, purveyed a system of literary criticism that devalued the
authority of the text and shifted it to the commentator.

The anti-Semitic ideas expressed by de Man in these early
writings are curiously like the one Eliot embodied in *After Strange
Gods:* Jews cannot be incorporated into Western civilization.
Eliot's "freethinking" Jews are very much like the Jews deplored by
de Man. I am indebted to Geoffrey Hartman's essay in *The New
Republic* for these quotations from de Man's early suppressed
work. "De Man posits a proper tradition. . . ." writes Hartman,
"marked by 'deep spiritual sincerity,' and then a second strain."
Those who follow the second strain, de Man wrote, are "aber-
rant," a "degeneration," and "mainly non-Germanic, specifically
Jews."

De Man held that if "a solution of the Jewish problem" removed Jews from Europe, this "would not result, for the literary
life of the West, in regrettable consequences. The latter would lose,
all in all, some people of mediocre value, and would continue as in
the past to develop according to its own great laws of evolution."

One supporter of the Eliot commemorative fund, a Jew, is the
present treasurer of the London Library. Eliot was himself chair-
man of the Library from 1952 to 1964. In a *Times* interview in
support of Eliot, the treasurer pointed out that Eliot "mentions
with great respect" the Jewish writer, Simone Weil. The connection
is worth comment.

It is true that Eliot greatly admired Simone Weil in her tormented search for the roots of Christian belief. Born a Jew and
violently anti-Semitic, Weil, like de Man, and like Eliot, mused in
her journals on what Western civilization would lose without the
Jews. Not much, she concluded.

Weil wanted in fact to subtract the Jewish component from
Christianity, and as a result could find no one to convert her, her
Christian ideas being too heretically against the Hebraic strain in
Christianity. Weil sought martyrdom, but managed, because her
parents had taken her out of the country, to bypass the kind suffered by Jews. Instead, she inflicted cigarette burns on her body,
and died of self-imposed starvation in 1945 in order to express
solidarity, as she said, with the suffering of French workers. Suffer-

ing and self-abnegation were Weil's chosen path, and she is called a saint by her many admirers. But how can one be a saint and at the same time an anti-Semite, as if spiritual endeavor had no substantive points of reference?

How can one be a poet of moral grandeur and write anti-Semitic lines, as if the values of poetry were made up merely of form, language, music, as if content had nothing to do with how we evaluate the poem? Such a position would mean that the community of poets, far from being Shelley's "unacknowledged legislators of the world," must in fact be barred from that post, limited to an appreciation of the surface beauty of art, more like hairdressers than poets, praising the perm without caring what's inside the do.

Amidst Eliot's nihilistic images—"Thoughts of a dry brain in a dry season"—there are hints of redemption. From "Burnt Norton," for example, earliest of the *Four Quartets:* "The moment in the rose-garden"; "the pool filled with water out of sunlight"; "In light upon the figured leaf"; "at the still point, there the dance is"; "a grace of sense, a white light still and moving." In these glimpses of elegant pattern and form lie hints of the divine order which, in the Eliotic grammar, translates into high Christian culture, from which the Jew is forever excluded.

After his marriage at age sixty-eight to a woman less than half his age, Eliot mellowed. With his young wife at his side, Eliot was transformed to a benign presence. He exchanged puns with Groucho Marx, who found him "a dear man," shed benignity on public occasions, and by dropping former friends, succeeded in severing himself from association with the old misanthropic framework. This was not the Christian *agape* he had sought all his life, but it was transformation by love all the same, by earthly love for his thirty-year-old secretary "whose eyes filled with adoration whenever they lit on him." (Groucho Marx again.)

During this period, when the 92nd Street YM&YWHA Poetry Center was directed by John Malcolm Brinnin, William Kolodney, educational director of the Y, wrote to Eliot in 1953 asking him to make a "brief statement" against Soviet anti-Semitism. Eliot must have sat down to it on the day he received the request, for his reply came within the week, and it goes far beyond the modest request. "A mere expression of agreement with 'a public stand against the present anti-Semitic policy of the Soviet government' is not enough," Eliot wrote, "for what decent individual could decline to support such a protest?

Eliot supplies what appears to him enough, adding almost fulsomely his analysis and abhorrence of anti-Semitism. "It is a symptom of profound difficulty, disorder and maladjustment in the economy and in the spiritual life of that nation. . . ." He compares, unasked, Russian anti-Semitism with the anti-Semitism of Hitler's Germany. The Russians, he says, are shrewder about covering their tracks. "The Nazis persecuted Jews for being Jews, and thereby incurred at once the antipathy of all civilised people. The Russians refrain from any overt doctrine of racial superiority, which would too flatly contradict their supposed principles. . . ." Eliot concludes resoundingly: "Any government which persecutes and stigmatises any body of its own nationals—and most notably the Jews—will in the end have to pay the full penalty for so doing. . . ."

Two things are notable about the letter. Eliot is careful this time to capitalize Jew, and he makes no mention of his own time of "difficulty, disorder and maladjustment" during which he wrote overtly anti-Semitic lines into his poems. The religious penitent, sufferer, and seeker of expiation for his own life-crimes missed an opportunity here to confess and repudiate what was already public knowledge anyway. Eliot, the genius of many selves, condemns anti-Semitism as if it had been perpetrated entirely by others.

How, then, should we respond to Eliot? How, in fact, should Eliot be taught to successive generations? Issue a warning with the poems as in a pack of cigarettes? Should we make use of Eliot's own prediction at the close of his letter to the director of the Y, and include it like a surgeon-general's notice? *Whoever engages in anti-Semitism* "will in the end have to pay the full penalty for so doing. . . ."

Eliot's old age brought him an apotheosis of late-in-life personal happiness. Readers may want to sympathize with belated joy that comes to a fellow human being. But it is also necessary to note that by then the damage was done. The poems of anti-Semitism and misogyny, the poisonous opinions, were carved into the canon to be read, as things stand now, without mitigating commentary for as long as Eliot is taught to the impressionable young.

The world has forgiven Eliot for writing well. It falls to those who are willing to risk it (not only Jews, one hopes), to protest to the world that a writer cannot be great so long as anti-Semitism mars the work. No more can an individual said to have climbed to sainthood be considered a saint while anti-Semitism mars his or her soul.

These are not new insights. What is new—or would be, if we could bring ourselves to it—is to act on these insights, to proclaim what we know: Whoever tries to discount the importance of anti-Semitism in a work of art severs idea from act, form from content, thought from feeling—those elements that may not be severed without severe deformation to the work. Can the elite in the Jew refrain from aligning itself with the elite in Eliot? Can battered Jewish self-esteem forbear from picking from the ground fragments of insignias dropped there by contemptuous Gentiles?

What would Eliot be to us then? A highly interesting writer, perhaps, who labored mightily to open a stunted vision into the grandeur of spiritual transcendence, but who failed to achieve his end. He never renounced or worked through his contempt. He merely began to affirm other things, a man of nearly seventy who escaped from his old intellectual friends, married a fresh young woman, and began to bask in being happy.

Forgiveness of those who write well is not the point. Seeing them with continuous clarity is.

—1989

Hunting Metaphors and Nazis

Frederick Busch's fictions, widely praised for their clarity and dignity, celebrate rural life in New England and the Midwest. In *Invisible Mending,** Mr. Busch gives us something else—Zimmer, New York Jew and first-person narrator, whose voice is nervous, sentimental, wisecracking, garrulous. "Can I come home?" is the plea Zimmer recalls from his panicked childhood; the phrase applies as well to the forty-year-old Zimmer's present plight. He has a wife, a son, an editor's job in a publishing house, but he still feels lost.

Zimmer is just Zimmer; he has no other name, and even this one is not authentic, having been altered after family immigration. Not to put too fine a point on it, *"Zimmer"* means "room" in German but Zimmer doesn't want to be squeezed into a room. Room is what Zimmer wants, room in the world; Zimmer doesn't like being a Jew.

"Inauthentic Jews," Jean-Paul Sartre wrote in "Anti-Semite and Jew," "are men whom other men take for Jews and who have decided to run away from this insupportable situation." This seems a fair description of Zimmer. When Zimmer was a boy, his assimilated, liberal parents bad-mouthed Jews and gave him Christmas, but Zimmer has to reject them anyway when he marries the gentile Lillian and adopts her family, "with their gold hair and delicate cheekbones," in place of "those squat and un-Americanized" people from whom he sprang.

Zimmer's marriage to Lillian and his subsequent fathering of their son, to whom he now in turn gives Christmas, are acts with which no champion of free choice would wish to quarrel. Zimmer's relationship to the Holocaust, however, is another matter. Before Lillian, there had been Rhona, a Jewish lover who introduced him to the Holocaust to win back his "Jewish soul."

---

*David R. Godine, 1984.

Though years later Zimmer still can't decide whether it was "sex or history that drove me on," he embarked on a tormented reading of Holocaust books and let Rhona drag him into a humiliating Nazi hunt. The outcome (it's all right to reveal it because the reader knows long before Rhona, who refuses to see copious clues) is that the "Nazi" turns out to be a Jewish refugee, "You were loving death," Zimmer accuses Rhona. "You love the God of the Jews in the deaths of the Jews." The confrontation with Rhona frees him to go off and find Lillian, who can be counted on for cool love and American baseball.

Because Zimmer is so dedicated a narrator-rememberer and Mr. Busch so skillful a novel constructor, the story can slip from past to present and back again (sometimes dizzyingly), cantilevering its way across decades. The technique creates a simultaneity of mood and event that keeps Zimmer's ambiguities always before us. It also keeps authorial stance obscured. At what ironic distance from himself does Mr. Busch want us to read about his character Zimmer, who must make farce of the Holocaust in order to rid himself of it? Whatever signposts the author provides are ambiguous.

When, after twelve years of marriage, Zimmer leaves Lillian and their beloved eight-year-old son, his reasons are fuzzy. And the tone is uncertain: The poor little overdetermined boy cries out in what sounds like parody, "Do we still get to have Christmas, Daddy?" The breakup mainly seems to occur so Zimmer can re-encounter Rhona and reconfirm his choice of Lillian. Rhona obliges with more farce. She has been cured of her Nazi obsession, she tells Zimmer, by marriage to a Turkish-Armenian Jew who grotesquely acts out *his* obsession with his former persecutors.

In place of obsession, Zimmer looks for the single idea that will be a shortcut to meaning and exclaims about this or that event that it would make "a dandy metaphor." He finds what he seeks on a tailor shop window. "Invisible mending" becomes his metaphor for what love can do when applied to the world's sorrows. Even Lillian feels moved to remind him that "invisible mending" won't work if the Ku Klux Klan takes over America. "The only place where you can run to . . . is Israel. . . . Home for the Jews? Remember?"

Zimmer is not without his charm, not the least of which is that he is the first to tell us the bad news about himself. What he seems not to know is that he suffers from the emotional thinness of someone who can believe in nothing but language. When he looks at "I Never Saw Another Butterfly," a book of poems and drawings done by children in the Terezin concentration camp, he thinks, "They were children of language," before emotion seizes him and he hurls the book away.

Zimmer's responses rebound off bad-taste jokes about Jews, and "leather-faced Hadassah ladies" come in for many a jibe. When he tells Lillian about Rhona's attempt to capture his "Jewish soul," Zimmer reports that this otherwise intelligent woman comments, "It's not that different from the usual Jewish Princess pact, is it?"

Talk about belatedness! What are these smugly mummified comments doing here if Zimmer is as jazzily up-to-date as he thinks? The answer is, he's not. For all his rushing about, Zimmer is as isolated from true encounter as a man locked in a room.

Having learned about Nazis, Zimmer feels free to quip about Abraham's binding of Isaac: "He was only obeying orders." Yet Zimmer also tries to get his firm to publish the poems of the Holocaust poet Paul Celan. Where lines from Celan's "Death-fugue" appear, they flood the pages with a tragic grandeur that all but drowns Zimmer's voice. It is as if Zimmer—or his author— had remembered that biblical Jews sometimes wrestled with angels and came away with new identities and names.

Mr. Busch lavishes language on Zimmer but never gives him a first name or a completed identity or a clear relationship to the moral implications of his own story. When the reader's mind (fatally for the novel) wanders outside this fiction to recall that there are real Nazis and real Nazi-hunters whose "paranoia" is justified, the novel shrinks to a nursery fictional world shielded from the terrors of the actual one where the mountain of Holocaust documentation yearly looms higher and where Jew and Christian alike struggle with agonized questions at the heart of their post-Holocaust relationship.

—1984

"I Had the Distinct Impression Death Was Jewish": E. L. Doctorow

I am not among those reviewers of E. L. Doctorow's *World's Fair** who want to take the author to task (the *New York Times Book Review,* the *New York Review of Books*) for passing off as novel a book that seems essentially memoir. The opposite view holds for me: Doctorow's skill at securing readers by evocation alone, without aids of plot or suspense, inspires my admiration. And yet I find curious unintended ironies in the book's very quietness.

At first the experience of reading *World's Fair* is like the slow licking of an ice-cream cone on a warm day: we stroll along, licking the cone, while our eyes rove lazily here and there—nothing need be intense while one is licking an ice-cream cone. Despite its lack of novelistic carrot-on-stick, *World's Fair* is made freshly readable by its narrating technique—here through the innocent eyes of young Edgar, who relates his boy's view of the years before World War II, culminating in a grand finale visit to the World's Fair of 1939.

The narrator is a sheltered, cherished Jewish boy for whom the important events of life are still domestic. He is allowed to perceive only dimly the family's economic distress during the Depression of the 1930s. Through the occasional narrative assistance young Edgar receives from his mother, Rose, and from his older brother, Donald, both of whom bear the same names in life as in fiction, additional stresses are made known. Sometimes, at the close of an incident related by young Edgar, a grown-up narrator summarizes and comments. But much is left uncommented on. The pattern seems to be that the seemingly trivial incidents rate a grown-up comment, to help us understand the depth of their resonance in the

---

*Random House, 1985.

life, while the more overt or active occurrences are often left unre-
marked.

Yet when the book is done and we understand what it is we
have been looking at, the question poses itself: what can this lack
of intensity mean? For what we, licking and strolling, have been
shown is nothing less than another piece belonging to the crazy
quilt of that intense genre, Jewish Boyhood in America. Compared
to the anguish of Henry Roth's *Call It Sleep,* to the fury of Philip
Roth's *Portnoy's Complaint,* this is tame boyhood indeed.

Instead of Portnoy's middle-class Jewish New Jersey, Doctorow
gives us a middle-class Jewish home in the West Bronx, but a home
devoid of rebellion or parental critique. Instead of stridency and
satire, rebellion or raucousness, he offers a sweetly flavored
nostalgia. *World's Fair,* the book whose action moves it toward the
Fair's City of the Future, leads its readers, in a reverse movement,
into a past whose landscapes—the schoolyards of the Bronx, the
father's record store, the mother's kitchen, Aunt Frances's decorous
seder in the wealthy goyish lotusland of Westchester—are all suf-
fused in the glow not only of what is gone, but of what is dead.

For Doctorow, one deduces from this book, the Jewish component can be portrayed as belonging entirely to the past; it is history; it neither poses a threat nor exerts a pull; its challenge is non-
present; it belongs to the precincts of tranquility and nostalgia,
that ice-cream-sweet embalming of what is dead.

In a writer's struggle to achieve balance between the
individual-particular on the one hand and its subsuming in the
archetypal-thematic on the other, Doctorow leans heavily toward
the second, in some books giving outlines, only, of character, as in
the old daguerrotypes of *Ragtime.* The technique of *World's Fair* is
close to that simple character-outlining. This mythologizing of
character (a form of stereotyping, in fact) gives great reassurance
and pleasure to readers of popular fiction: ground once gripped
doesn't shift under your feet.

Yet if we take for the moment as our touchstone Coleridge's
still-useful dictum that poetry ought to make the strange familiar
and the familiar strange and apply it to a writer's obligation not
only to enrich the present by distancing it but also to make the past
more present, then the criticism one can make of the techniques of
Ragtime and *World's Fair* is that they start with what is remote and

make it remoter. The inevitable loss of individuality is an odd thing in itself, since Doctorow has said he perceives the present political danger to be that "the moral immensity of the single soul is in question." Often the individual in these novels is endangered by the novelist's technique—characters are endearing, but quaint, remote, ultimately miniaturized.

Here is an example of the child's story-book prose in which Doctorow describes the annual family trip, via streetcar, to the seder:

> Aunt Frances greeted us with a smile at the door. Behind her was her full-time maid, Clara, a tall, angular black woman who wore a white uniform with matching white shoes. Clara took our coats and bundles. To our surprise and delight, my habitually late father was already there. He had come up from Grand Central Station on the New York Central. "You're late," he said. "What took you so long!" And everyone laughed.

In *World's Fair* the familiar Jewish-American cultural progression from something to nothing is made plain, albeit in the book's pervasive quiescent tone, without complaint, grief, or anger. In the absence of positive Jewish teaching young Edgar draws the following inferences:

> I had the distinct impression death was Jewish. It had happened to my grandma, who spoke Jewish [*sic*], and everyone had immediately repaired to the synagogue. A memorial candle in a glass now stood flickering on the kitchen table for Grandma, whom I had seen light similar candle glasses for her own dead. Hebrew letters were on the glass label as on the window of the chicken market where dead chickens hung on hooks by their feet, some plucked, some half plucked, some with all their feathers. Chickens, I knew, were Jewish. . . .

And again:

> Of course I knew virtually nothing about religion. . . . I knew so far that most of the Jewish holidays were not as much fun as the regular ones. There was some forced insistence behind them. . . .

Yet though Edgar escapes the yoke of religion, this boy's life is no *Huckleberry Finn,* either. Little Edgar is by no means free to adventure in America. He is a timid worrier, a weak, loved child, prone to car sickness, colds, and crying. He reads a lot. His narrat-

ing voice is slow, grave, at times replacing the ingenue fairy-tale
tone with a voice somewhat elderly:

> At midnight I tiptoed down the hall to the living room and I
> found Donald asleep on the sofa in front of the radio, which was
> still playing. The broadcast was from Times Square. Crowds
> cheered, horns blew, and the announcer interviewed people who
> shouted their greetings into the microphone. It was 1937. I
> looked out the window. Eastburn Avenue was dark. I hoped my
> parents would be home soon. Happy New Year, I said to myself,
> and went back to bed.

A tour of the Fair's buildings is presented as the structural
climax of the book, though it is not the center of its meaning. The
City of the Future is dutifully savored by young Edgar, who wins
tickets for the whole family by writing an essay on the theme of
"the typical American boy" (. . ."If he is Jewish he should say so"
is inspired by his having denied his Jewishness when assaulted by
toughs in a strange neighborhood). But the symbolic, hence emotional, hence *real* climax occurs in a sleazy sideshow to which
Edgar's young girlfriend and her mother take him. They are gentiles and their lives appear interestingly irregular to the boy: Edgar
has to undergo a severe grilling by his mother before she'll allow
him to accompany them. The two mothers are poles apart: Edgar's
is doting and demanding, imposing strict rules and expecting great
results; the gentile mother is relaxed, easygoing, and ultimately
leads Edgar into an initiation.

As if Edgar's mother possessed prophetic powers, it turns out
that the gentile mother whom she is so loathe to let her son accompany is engaged in unsavory employment at the Fair: she performs
in a tank of water, swimming in and out of the clutches of an
amorous octopus who finally rips off her bathing suit.

After this moment, the metaphor for *World's Fair,* that record
of a boy's progress toward the promise of his own future in America, must change to become something quite different from a stroll
through a pleasant past sweetened by licks of a melting ice-cream
cone. For when our own glance rounds the curve of time into the
present, the novels we see emerge from the pen of grownup Edgar
Doctorow—*Welcome to Hard Times, The Book of Daniel, Ragtime, Loon Lake*—are those in which an American past is translated into a roster of mythological figures: frontier settler, union

organizer, union buster, revolutionary, reformer, self-made millionaire, and Lower East Side Jew who invents his way out of the ghetto.

The grownup Jewish man in present time, feeling the pressure of his own past as something to rail against (like Roth), or acknowledge as a shaper of intellect and sensibility (like Bellow and, to a lesser extent, Malamud) does not exist. We see that the City of the Future that was the highlight of young Edgar's Fair could hold no place for Jews. We see that a Jewish past construed as entirely nostalgic forwards no freight into the present. And we see that a slow swim through a tank of murky water, in which an octopus reaches out and snatches off your clothes, can become both metaphor and parable for the entry into mainstream culture by an American *yingele* from whom former Jewish identity has been stripped away.

—1986

Norman Mailer's Holocaust-Poisoned Jews

In the matter of anti-Semitic portraits, Shakespeare's Shylock is probably as sympathetic and enlightened as we can hope to have. Shakespeare's Jew is not demonic: he is governed by cause and effect. His poisoned soul has its reasons. Shylock suffers at the hands of gentiles, and when he finds his own hand strengthened he becomes the horror we know—demander of his pound of flesh.

Four centuries later American Jews are being warned that the Holocaust has hardened Jewish hearts: Jews are in danger of losing compassion, neglecting the suffering of others, and seeking revenge against the world. This view, which effects a kind of wholesale transformation of Jews into Shylocks, assures that those who were victims once can count on being victims again. First because of the blows taken, second because of what the blows are said to have done. Once again, goes this libel, Jews have poisoned the wellsprings of fellow feeling.

The accuser this time is Norman Mailer, who takes the matter right into the presidential campaign.* If Jews don't nominate the Reverend Jesse Jackson for President it's not because they've thought anything through, but rather because "Hitler succeeded in smashing . . . generosity of spirit." As Mailer sees it, the souls of Jews may be so poisoned that they will dodge the opportunity to vote for Jackson, who will "give young black people the confidence that American society exists also for them" and "open a great counterattack against the metastases of the drug problem."

Mailer indicts Jews for being narrowly hung up on a few Jewish concerns vis-à-vis Jackson: the "Hymietown" insult (Mailer reminds us that Jackson apologized); the connections to Farrakhan

---

* Op-Ed, *New York Times,* April 18, 1988.

and Arafat (though Jackson has repudiated neither one, Mailer calls us to appreciate that Jackson has dissociated from both); and the disquieting stance on Israel (Mailer consoles with a rotundity of prose: a candidate for president of the United States carries little weight "against the multitudinous labyrinths and floodgates of . . . history").

Mailer looks for transcendence of these minor matters. He develops his thesis: "Since World War II, I have lived, like every other Jew, with the fundamental ill of the Holocaust. Hitler succeeded in wiping out more than one-third of the Jewish population in the world, and upon the rest of us he left a fearful curse: the legacy of Nazism, now in its fifth decade, is still there to poison one's finer moral substance."

Leaving aside the question of whether this is the first time Mailer has used the word "us" in connection with Jews, we can move to a more urgent question: Is it this determinism, this poisonous reaction-formation, that prevents the finer moral substance of Jews from voting for Jackson for president? Or is it something fresh and powerful, like thought?

Mailer yearns back to the time when "the welfare of all the people of the world came before our own [that is, Jews'] welfare." After we fight free of the fumes of Mailer's fantasy, let us ask him this question: What religion (let alone political system) counsels us to love our neighbor better than ourselves, or "before" ourselves? As *well as* ourselves is good enough for Hillel and Jesus.

If Mailer offers counsel not of this world and not of any angels' world either, what world are we in? Why—back in his old one of "The White Negro," famously described by him in an essay published in *Dissent* in 1957 and reprinted two years later in *Advertisements for Myself*. It was there that Mailer first swept from Holocaust to "Negro": "Probably, we will never be able to determine the psychic havoc of the concentration camps. . . ."

The only right responder for Mailer was that existential harrower of hell, the hipster. The hipster's unconventional wisdom derived from the Negro, in whom "psychopathy is most prevalent. . . . And in the worst of perversion, promiscuity, pimpery, drug addiction, rape, razor-slash, bottle-break, what-have-you, the Negro discovered and elaborated a morality of the bottom. . . ."

From there the sainted soul of the hipster soared upward, like St. Anthony's when he was among the temptations.

As then, so now. Thirty years later, Mailer is swinging round again with another apocalypse, another salvational theory out of the Negro. Then it was the generic Negro, from which the hipster White Negro derived. Now it is Jesse Jackson, whose faults are to be forgotten in the grand apotheosis of his surreal and sainted powers.

What a melancholy distance Mailer has traversed! He calls on the Negro now to cure us of the very things he once told us the Negro brought to liberate: drugs, psychopathic rebellion, and existential swinging.

And with what carefree cheerfulness Mr. Mailer votes his emotions! The romancer in him changes the venue: if he's not voting for soul he's voting for style. He remembers how he felt about John Kennedy. "A man . . . young, ambitious, with a taste for adventure. . . . He was not perfect, our Jack, but he brought light into the lives of my generation."

"Our Jack" turned out to be in fact less trustworthy in personal and political life than many expected, and was the one, after all, who sharply escalated the number of troops sent as ill-advised "advisers" into Vietnam.

The White Negro. The saint. These bring to mind another Jew obsessed with saints—Simone Weil—though by a path very different from the engorgements of Mailer-culture. Hers was the way of abnegation, self-denial, and, ultimately, self-starvation. During the years of the Holocaust, she sought self-sacrifice and identification with French workers through long factory hours and less than wartime rations, taking a longer way round to martyrdom than if she had declared herself a Jew in Vichy France.

Mailer, too, seeks solidarity with the poor and oppressed. He lectures Jews on the quality of mercy, playing Portia to their Shylock. Indeed, in his Op-Ed piece he describes Jews—who have been living in the dialectic of judgment and mercy since the first psalm—as having "descended" lower than Shylock, who at least, for Mailer, had the human trait of "being able to bleed."

"What made us great as a people," writes Mailer in the *Times*, "is that we, of all ethnic groups, were the most concerned with the world's problems." One day, when Mailer's knowledge of Jews goes back further than the civil-rights movement of the sixties, he will discern other claims to greatness. Meanwhile: "The psychopath murders . . . ," says the White Negro, "out of the necessity to purge his violence, for if he cannot empty his hatred then he cannot love. . . ."

In his rush to transcendence, Mailer seeks out energy-bestowing substances: a psychopath or a fantasy-Negro; just now, only Jesse Jackson will do. Not "getting there" but *being there* appears to be Mailer's goal; not working through to hard-won ground of social, political, and economic betterment, but Tarzaning onto it is his notion of the existential leap: giant steps in the children's game of "May I."

In his search for the redeeming Negro, hipster, swinger, bottomed-out moral man, Mailer comes up with an endorsement, as once he endorsed hipster-psychopaths and the killer Jack Henry Abbott, of whom Mailer fervently wrote in *In the Belly of the Beast:* "A potential leader, a man obsessed with a vision of more elevated human relations in a better world. . . ."

Woe to a world of such apocalyptic visions from such a counselor to the Jews.

—1988

The Fate of Anne Frank's Diary

Why is Anne Frank's diary so treasured throughout the world, translated into fifty different languages, presented in stage dramatizations to wide acclaim, and nowhere more so than in Germany?

In an important way, Anne Frank's diary, just as much as it is a Holocaust book, is also a charming story of The Little Family in the Secret Annex, hidden cozily together there—mother, father, and two fond sisters. There is even a little love episode with a boy Anne's age, whose awkward parents have come along into hiding too, plus a sour bachelor dentist, all of whom provide comic effect and the give-and-take of their small society.

Outside the cozy hiding place stalk wicked men, but inside are games, learning, flirtation, a father to advise, a mother to rebel against—the Family Romance intact and, during the writing of the diary, nestled safe. Nothing really bad has happened yet to those in hiding: only quarrels that are patched up, food and clothing shortages that are ingeniously resolved, fears of discovery that turn out to be false. There is only adversity, that evil of the coherent world, which virtue and character meet and master every day. Why shouldn't the world love such a story?

In the 1950s, shortly after Anne's diary was originally published, I was drawn to attend a discussion on the phenomenon of evil by a group of Jungian psychologists. After listening for a bit, I was astonished to realize that the participants were not, as I expected, referring to Hitler, the Holocaust, and the murder of Europe's Jews. Instead, they spoke of what might be called "uplifting" evil, the kind found in folktales, where it hatches heroic strengths: thwarted quests draw forth ingenuity; the need of rescue recruits extra courage.

I remember inwardly protesting: But that's just *ordinary* evil, and the proof is that it is overcome by steadfastness and virtue. If that's what they call evil, what language is left to describe what happened in the Holocaust?

"I . . . feel so strong . . . I can bear a great deal," is a line familiar to us from Anne Frank's diary. "I don't think I shall easily bow down before the blows that inevitably come to everyone."

One doesn't for a moment doubt her, or the pathos of that youthful self-belief. The blows that inevitably come to everyone she would surely have mastered, absorbed, transcended— whatever it is that strong people do.

Nothing makes us see so plainly as Anne's diary the radical disjunction between "the blows of life"—to be met with character, fortitude, religious faith, ingenuity, courage—and what happened in the Holocaust, against which no greatness of spirit or character could prevail, and from which a random wind carried a straggling remnant.

Over seven hundred pages long, *The Critical Edition of Anne Frank's Diary* was prepared by the Netherlands State Institute for War Documentation.* It consists of details about the betrayal of the Frank family (the identity of their Dutch betrayer is still unknown); the arrest and deportation of Anne and her family; some discussion of the adaptation of the diary into a play and the old Meyer Levin charges that his version was scrapped in favor of a more universalist one; a section called "Attacks on the Authenticity of the Diary"; and the diary itself, in three versions.

After the people living in the Secret Annex were arrested and taken away, the place was ransacked, but the greatest treasure overlooked: among the books and papers dumped on the floor, the two Dutch friends who had cared for the hidden families found Anne's diary.

Anne kept her diary from June 12, 1942, through August 1, 1944. She filled it with remarkable observations on life in the Secret Annex at 263 Prinsengracht in Amsterdam, and on what she learned of the terrifying world outside it. Even her own teenage passions come under her writer's scrutiny with innate style and unfailing wit. When all the adults in their hiding place grow impatient with her "cheeky" high spirits, this girl so starved for the feel

---

*Doubleday, 1990.

of the outdoors can write: "The rain of rebukes dies down to a light summer drizzle."

Because of Anne's gift, human reality is bestowed upon a handful of people who might otherwise have died into the mind-numbing statistics of the Holocaust. Their terror, exhaustion, and illness as they were later dragged from camp to camp is not hard to imagine, and the dealt-out deaths from which they ultimately perished alert the heart in some fresh and terrible way.

After Anne's last August entry, she was taken to Westerbork, and from there transported to Auschwitz-Birkenau. In the last months, with the SS in disarray before Allied advances, yet still grasping their booty of captives to be disposed of according to the will of the Third Reich, Anne and her sister Margot were sent with a transport of women crammed into cattle trucks to Bergen-Belsen, her death-place eight months later in March 1945. Of the eight who had been in hiding, only Anne's father, Otto Frank, held onto life. He was responsible for the publication of the diary after the war ended, and in a way is responsible again for the appearance of the present edition.

Otto Frank willed Anne's diary manuscript to The Netherlands State Institute for War Documentation, and one year after his death in 1979 the editors began to conceive of this mammoth volume. It had become clear, the editors tell us, that because of "the growing number of slurs" and doubts cast "on the personal integrity of the author and on the relationship between the original manuscript, the published version, and its many translations . . . ," they ought to bring out this volume.

Differences among the three diary texts are small. We can now see in what way the version originally published by Anne's father, Otto Frank, slightly bowdlerized Anne's text by the removal of some of her early sexual explorations (they offended the Christian sensibilities of the Dutch, we are told) and by the excision of youthful outbursts against other family members and friends in their cramped hiding place.

Anne's second version is a polishing, sometimes to achieve a more grownup tone, which the reader certainly doesn't require. "Much as I don't like to," becomes in one case, for example, "albeit unwillingly." There are other self-improving alterations that have nothing to do with the impact of the diary on the reader, but everything to do with Anne's conscious concern for clarity or style, her full-hearted embrace, at age fourteen, of her goal of becoming a writer.

Anne's two versions offer proof where no further proof was needed: she was a real writer, absorbed in the task of translating her world into words. The publishers see this new edition as a vindication of Anne and quote her: "I want to go on living even after my death!" Now she will live, say the publishers—in this big, weighty, expensive, annotated edition.

To some it may feel like a hateful book, symbol of a shocking need to reply to charges of the self-styled "revisionists"—in plain English, those who deny the Holocaust happened. People both crazy and cruel, in other words, demented and demonic, who have provided themselves with an abstruse-sounding category to belong to. Revisionists. Who say Anne Frank's diary is a fraud.

For me one of the most disturbing parts of the book is called "Document Examination and Handwriting Identification of the Text Known as the Diary of Anne Frank: Summary of Findings." Handwriting experts have had to prove that Anne's diary is not a fake despite the discrepancies among Anne's original, revised, and father-edited texts, which are no more—in fact, far less—than the usual differences to be found among the revised drafts of any writer's work. And so the three variorum texts are printed in triple alignment, the descenders and ascenders of Anne's handwriting are magnified and measured, the spacing arrangements and ink impressions on the pages are studied for symmetries, the postmarks on her letters examined to determine if they were actually sent through the mails in order to compose comparison standards with the writing in her diary, the changes in Anne's penmanship are explained by psychological experts in the handwriting of the young, and so on.

In the end the hope of accounting for discrepancies among the editions is of course thwarted, for even in this presentation there are still names and incidents which some of the living (one of them is Otto Frank's second wife) do not wish to see revealed, and so again there are lacunae. How can this matter? Enemies of the Jews, quick as Balaam to curse, will not see what is there to see even if their mounts rear up and throw them to the ground.

I must depart here from print and move to a recent televised documentary by the Dutch filmmaker Willy Lindwer, who interviewed several women once interned as teenagers in the camps where Ann was imprisoned and perished, and who witnessed her ordeal there.

They describe, among other brutalities, the transfer to Bergen-Belsen, some of it on foot, in bitter storming weather. Anne and her sister Margot are by then both skeletal, the skin of their faces like thin leather, as one woman describes it, clinging to the bones. In the last stages of typhus, they are standing naked under a bit of blanket, in mud, under a torrential freezing rain.

One woman now in her sixties seems to be reexperiencing shock when she tells how, as a sheltered adolescent girl just arrived at the camp, she had to undress before the guards and submit to the shaving of her body hair. Another tells of being stripped, but of clinging to a last garment she calls a menstruation girdle, only to have it ripped from her body by an SS guard. "Nothing more can happen to me," she had thought in horror.

Now Anne, who had written that she still believed people were good at heart, sees it all, all there is to see, this young girl so eager for experience. If she could have kept her diary there in hell, what belief would she have recorded? Can we project Anne into the future? Suppose she had lived? Would she, like Primo Levi, have continued to write graceful books to salvage and understand the lives of those who did not survive? Like the life of her beloved sister Margot, for one, who is described by a survivor as having fallen dead one night from the bunk shared with Anne, to smash upon the cement floor? And then one day might Anne, like Levi, have hurled herself down a staircase to dash the no-longer-bearable images from her brain?

History is an accounting which life appears to be constantly trying to renegotiate, and nothing could be more acid-cut proof of it than this swollen tome which has at its heart the slender sayings a murdered girl set down.

I propose another kind of publishing venture. It would be a volume nearly as slim as Anne's original diary, but would join that manuscript to the testimony of ordeals these women shared with Anne, and to what they witnessed of her dying in Auschwitz and Bergen-Belsen.

Disseminate that volume around the world, dramatize it on the stages of Germany and Holland. Only then will we have the complete and annotated book: *Anne Frank, Her Diary & Death.*

—1990

Justice for Jonah, or, a Bible Bartleby

Show me a text that speaks of God's unbounded mercy, and images of the Holocaust appear before my eyes. It's not anything I can help. *Theology* doesn't help. This is visceral. I don't imagine I'm alone in this. Perhaps my generation will have to die out in the desert before God can appear again on an untarnished mercy seat. Such a return is essential for the healthy nurture of the human religious impulse. I understand that. But I can't be of any help there.

Before the Holocaust it was possible for piety to say, as we read in Lamentations, "We are punished for our sins." After the Holocaust, none but a twisted piety dares say it.

How should someone like me read—as I do with fascination every Yom Kippur—the Book of Jonah?* Here, irony of ironies, is the man whose problem springs from his certainty that God will be merciful. Sure enough, when he is sent to prophesy doom to sinful Nineveh, God, as Jonah knew He would, rains down mercy instead of punishment, thus making Jonah a false prophet. Imagine! Jonah's is a theological problem for which the twentieth century has devised a complete solution, if Jonah only knew.

Every Yom Kippur I ask myself how Jonah would speak if he could somehow learn what happened to us. Mercy, pity, judgment, punishment: in what proportions might Jonah ascribe those attributes to God if he knew our condition? Is there some way to make a continuum of past and present, as if the Holocaust had not broken its back? Might Jonah study us with the same astonishment as we study him? Let us see what imagination will provide.

Meanwhile, here is Jonah. Thrown overboard. Swallowed by a fish. Brought back to his beginning, a still-reluctant prophet who hates the mercy meted out to a repentant people. God Himself

---

* The King James Version of the Bible used in this essay.

chides Jonah for his mean-spiritedness. Fetches up a vegetable-parable to fetch home the point of brotherly love and fatherly compassion.

Before he entered the biblical moment recounted in his book, the life of Jonah ben Amittai, the prophet, had been long and illustrious. Over the stormy waters flew the dove (Yonah) with truth (Amittai), the life-giving green of prophecy, in his mouth. Then Jonah stepped into the book of himself—and into the world of sermons, literature, historical anachronism, tall tales and fables, Christian fulminations against the Jews, and cautionary tales for Victorian children.

Other prophets speak to us. Not Jonah. Although he prophesied long and well, no one recorded his words. Only that single sentence to the people of Nineveh: "Yet 40 days and Nineveh shall be overthrown." What's recorded is biography. A scandalous episode in Jonah's life. When God called him to prophesy to Nineveh, Jonah ran away. As if Jonah's read Bernard Malamud's "The Jewbird": "I'm running. I'm flying [in this case, swimming], but I'm also running." Onto a ship that will take him as far from Nineveh as possible. Down to Tarshish, except that a storm interceded.

Why does a seasoned prophet balk at going forth to prophesy again? He is positive God will be merciful, and that he does not want. But in fact he will be hated whether judgment or mercy prevails, this bringer of bad news. "They hate him that rebuketh in the gate," says Amos. "And they abhor him that speaketh uprightly."

Think of the pain of trying to suppress prophecy. "I said, I will not make mention of him, nor speak any more in his name," Jeremiah confesses. "But his word was in my heart as a burning fire shut up in my bones, and I was weary with holding it in, and I could not."

Would any prophet enjoy not speaking? The choice is between fire and water. Jonah chose the sea.

And so Jonah suffers the name of "runaway," an *ad absurdum* satire on every prophet who ever protested unworthiness to carry the divine message. He is called the prophet who cared more for his own image (if, after his doom predictions, God shows mercy, won't Jonah appear to be a false prophet?) and for the image of the Jews (if the pagans of Nineveh repent, won't the stiff-necked Jews appear worse to God?), than for the truth which calls to him by name, and by whose name he is eponymously called.

And that's where Jonah stays stuck. He's the prophet who, according to Christian commentators, illustrates the narrowness and selfishness of the Jews. A few examples suffice:

"The unlovely character of the dour, recalcitrant Hebrew prophet . . . " (*The Interpreter's Dictionary of the Bible*). "A narrow-minded Israelite mentality . . . " (from a high-school text-book, *Teaching the Old Testament*).

Jewish interpreters have not departed much from Christian views, though naturally leaving out the anti-Semitic garnish. One guesses at a reason: though such commentary makes Jews and a Jewish prophet look bad, it makes what Christian commentators call the "Old Testament God" look good. Vindictive judgment, wrath, devouring punishments are banished. In their place, mercy, pity, love. To which Jonah so perversely objects.

Still, the question persists: How can Jonah, who believes in God's omnipotence, expect to hide from God? Is he deficient in understanding? The first in the line of brilliantly perceptive proph-ets to show dull-wittedness? Not at all. He does not mistake his own powerless position. He surely expects to be found. *Moby Dick* calls up a sermon on Jonah, but biblical Jonah is closer to Mel-ville's Bartleby, the scrivener, who prefers not to perform the duties for which he's engaged, even though he hasn't a shred of power or an ounce of right on his side. It makes us think that Jonah, like Bartleby, knows something. What that something is, in Jonah's case, I will later try to imagine, by means of a midrash of my own. For now, running away is part of Jonah's Bartlebyness. He, too, has no weapons or defense, but runs on without hope (Bartleby in-wardly; Jonah to the sea). When the storm overtakes his ship, Jonah is perfectly unsurprised and unfrantic. He will not pray. He can sleep, knowing that God is in pursuit and will surely find a means to reach him. But Jonah will not acquiesce in his fate.

In this mode, how Jonah has attracted the poets! Robert Frost takes him up in the verse play *A Masque of Mercy,* only to put him down with a New Testament judgment. A character aptly named Paul suggests a cure for Jonah's insistence on justice in "an oubliet-te, / Where you must lie in self-forgetfulness / On the wet flags before a crucifix. . . ."

In Paul Goodman's play *Jonah*, the prophet is an aging standup comic complete with nagging wife and a shrugging, "Who, me?" attitude. "Jonah," writes Goodman in a preface, "should have a slight Jewish accent throughout." Here he is, then, the original *schlemiel.* When God zigged, he zagged. God wishes for once to send down wholesale forgiveness, no questions asked, and Jonah objects. Not only Jonah, but God also is cartooned. No mystery here about God's intentions, just simple equations: sin plus repentance equals mercy. Like Frost, Goodman nudges Jonah toward a Christological exit from his dilemma. There will one day come good news, an angel confides.

As Jonah called out for justice, so his story calls out to us to bestow justice on Jonah—on this Bible Bartleby, who prefers not to. Since justice, however, is such a perilous matter, let's not approach it pell-mell, but return to other events of the story to see how they sharpen themselves, like Neptune's trident, to pierce Jonah's good name.

Even the pagan sailors on the ship bound for Tarshish behave better than Jonah. When the lot falls on him, he suggests they throw him overboard. The sailors are reluctant to carry this out. First, a midrash tells us, they dipped his feet, then his knees, then his hips. At each immersion the sea calmed, and so, sensible men at last, they relinquished their qualms, and Jonah, to the sea. Now an immense creature of the sea appears, popularly called a whale, but in Hebrew *dag gadol,* "a great fish." It slips over Jonah like a glove, but there's no trauma. Swallowed safe into the fish's belly, Jonah beautifully gives thanks:

> The waters compassed me about, even to the soul; the depth closed me round about, the weeds were wrapped about my head.
>   I went down to the bottoms of the mountains; the earth with her bars was about me for ever: yet hast thou brought up my life from corruption, O Lord my God.

But there is not a word about going forth to prophesy.

Of Jonah's three-day stay inside the fish, nothing else has been recorded in the text—no report from inside the fish. Yet, while the fish's eyes flashed like beacons, refracting light through giant lenses, and Jonah viewed a heaving universe, those two creatures, I believe, conversed. At first they were brief: "Don't cut me," said the fish. "Don't contract," said Jonah. That bargain is kept. Fish and man survive, for three days and nights, in perfect symbiotic balance. The all-important conversations that I believe ensued we will have to leave until later, for the fact is, Jonah was now *too* comfortable. So God (another midrash) sends a pregnant fish to which Jonah is transferred. There he felt the squeeze. There he learned what narrowness is.

Now Jonah goes to Nineveh. Aldous Huxley said that the people in El Greco's paintings look as if they've been inside the whale. We can imagine Jonah looking a little like them, thin and elongated, pressed within and without, stretched taut with anxiety: a touch of Giacometti there, too. Jonah pronounces the single sentence that sentences Nineveh to its doom: "Yet forty days and Nineveh shall be overthrown."

Everyone believes him. For a prophet worried about his credibility, it's simply outstanding. Everyone repents. The people of Nineveh fast and force their animals to fast, too, as if saying to God: If you don't notice suffering in us, maybe you'll notice it in them; or: If *you* won't show mercy, why should we? They put sackcloth not only on themselves, they dress their animals in it also. To the distractable mind this may add a kind of Beatrix Potter note: Mrs. Tiggy-winkle the hedgehog in her apron and mob cap, Peter Rabbit in his elegant vest, all doffed in favor of the new fashion—sackcloth, sackcloth everywhere.

As it turns out, there's shrewdness in this gesture by the evildoers of Nineveh. They know something about catching God's attention. In the final chiding of Jonah, God asks him how he could *not* spare Nineveh when it is so populous with people who "cannot discern between their right hand and their left hand; and," God uniquely adds, "also much cattle."

Compare and contrast Jonah however we will—to the sailors on the boat, to the fishes in the sea, to the worst abominators of the pagan world—Jonah comes out looking bad. And when in the end he watches from a distance to see what happens, and finds mercy pouring down on repentant Nineveh, Jonah, unregenerate, bursts out in anger: "O Lord, was this not my saying, when I was yet in my own country? Therefore I fled to Tarshish. . . ." God has to talk to him severely, and gets thereby some of the best lines in the Bible, although from Jonah's point of view there is a problem of logic.

I have spoken of calling for justice for Jonah. Yet how take kindly to the idea of a prophet who is so intent on principles of law that he can't unbend himself in the direction of mercy when it comes? To move closer to the goal, I propose we posit two Jonahs. Only one of these two Jonahs will need requitement of justice; the other can remain where we find him, thrown upon the world's mercy. (Though, like Portia judging Shylock, the world, scorning Jonah for his lack of mercy, subjects him to a judgment from which mercy is withheld.)

Still, why two Jonahs? First let me explain what is *not* the answer to that question. Freud posited two Moseses in *Moses and Monotheism,* claiming that the first one was killed in the desert and replaced by a second. Although Jonah's three days and nights in the belly of the fish could be reason enough for the death of Jonah One and replacement by Jonah Two, I don't mean there were actually two Jonahs. Nor do I intend to invoke that other ready response, "Why *not* two Jonahs (especially since there are already two fishes)?" There was really only one Jonah, but so changed by his experience in the fish as to have become practically another. (This seems as good a time as any to mention that certain historical discrepancies exist between the life of Jonah the man, generally located in the eighth century B.C.E., and the Book of Jonah, written probably in the fourth century B.C.E. One such discrepancy is that a later vocabulary appears in Jonah the book that Jonah the man couldn't have known. In this sense, of course, there *are* two Jonahs, the man and the book, but that is a very different sense from the one intended here.)

So: a before-the-fish Jonah and an after-the-fish Jonah.

Who was before-the-fish Jonah One? Not a nice fellow, says tradition, both Christian and Jewish, as we've seen. Before-the-fish Jonah One is narrow, without *understanding* of God's mercy and love, says tradition, but with, nonetheless, unabated faith in them. So much for Jonah One, whose problem, clearly, *stems* from his wholehearted belief in God's unfailing mercy.

After-the-fish Jonah Two was another matter. Here we can attempt some linking of past and present by arranging to have this man, of unshakable faith in God's mercy, see us in our post-Holocaust predicament.

Jonah himself brings us halfway to a solution. Like Bartleby, he knows something that makes him persist in flight against all odds. Whatever that something is (even if it is—*most certainly* if it is—despair), it is powerful enough to make him stand against the inevitable. What is it Jonah knows?

Let us try to imagine our way into Jonah's sojourn in the fish. This fish, Talmud tells us, was prepared at Creation for Jonah. The fish, we might say, is a kind of underwater angel, created to do God's bidding. Now let me posit my midrash. The fish has soaked up the events of the millennia. In those three days and nights in the womb of the deep, here is what must have happened. Like Milton's angel forecasting the future to Adam when paradise is lost, the fish reveals to Jonah what is to come. For three days and nights the fish presents scenes of time that will be. (Perhaps it is the pregnant fish, who, after all, must also have been prepared at Creation—an angel at God's bidding taking on the burdens of ichthyoid sex—who is the communicative one.) First there is the Babylonian exile: how the tongue of the sucking child cleaved to the roof of his mouth for thirst; how the young children asked for bread, and no one gave it to them; how skin was blackened like an oven, because of the terrible famine. "He hath broken my bones. . . . He hath bent his bow, and set me as a mark for the arrow. . . ." The fish's recitation of a few verses from Lamentations wonderfully concentrates Jonah's brain. After that, as in a kind of theater, the fish's cavernous interior fills with scenes from inquisitions and expulsions and ghettos and pogroms and, at last, death camps and crematoria. What the fish teaches Jonah is that, a mere twenty-five hundred years after his boat trip to Tarshish, the civilized world, carrying out with dispatch what gave the pagans pause, would fling six million Jonahs into the depths. The fish, eyes flashing like crystal globes, recounts everything. What the fish's stories tell is that there will be times—incredible as it must have seemed to the man of faith—when there will be no divine intervention, neither judgment nor mercy. Times for which new names will be learned: "eclipse of God," "a turning away of God's face."

Can it be right to say that after-the-fish Jonah wanted only judgment, not mercy? Perhaps he wanted more than that. Consistency. Judgment you could count on. A mercy that was meet. Wanted there never to be a time when there would be no judge and no judgment. If they are lacking, how can there be mercy?

Jonah is guilty of a terrible hubris: he becomes a would-be shaper of the world. Dissatisfied with the endings God provides, he wants to write his own ending to the Book of Jonah.

But God goes ahead with the ending we know.

By the time Jonah got to Nineveh, he was spewing out prophecy the way the fish spewed him. He was stuffed with Jewish history backward and forward the way the fish was stuffed with him. Exhausted, surfeited, he sinks down in his booth to watch the acting out of the last episode. The sun is hot. The desert wind abrasive. After three days in the fish, Jonah's skin is no doubt sensitive. He needs shade badly. God provides a *kikayon,* a gourd vine. Then God withers the vine.

Now comes the strangest bit of God-teasing. Jonah is a man in despair. He wants nothing for himself. A man who has had himself thrown into the sea and lived three days and nights in the belly of a fish who tells him everything there is in creation wants nothing. Except a little shade. Which God destroys, a last link in Jonah's chain of botched efforts.

And then this tease about a gourd. It's the oddest thing, God saying that Jonah *pities* the gourd because it's destroyed. "Thou hast had pity on the gourd, for which thou hast not labored, neither madest it grow; which came up in a night, and perished in a night. . . ." *Pity* for the gourd? We know what Jonah feels—it's *anger* at this last-straw loss of a convenience. Then the great point thundered home: "And should I not spare Nineveh, that great city . . . ?"

How shall we understand it—this equating of a gourd, which provides shade, with a people? Is this the *non sequitur* it seems? Or does God require the shelter of human beings against his own creation—good and evil, mercy and justice, reward and punishment, shall and shall not—all the hard edges of a moral world, shadowless, relentless as the blazing desert sun. Without the spreading penumbras of human response to soften that moral construct, does God grow faint?

Happily for Jonah, his glimpse into later centuries has not made of him a twentieth-century man. He is alive in an age of faith and could not conceive of replying in a nihilistic vein, as a twentieth-century being might: "Will you destroy the gourd again and again to make a point, as if it were no more to you than human life . . . which you created to make a point . . . which you preserve to make another . . . and permit, now and then, to be destroyed as if there were no point at all?"

All the same, Jonah is a monster. Among other monsters. He is sent to prophesy to Nineveh, a monster of a city. When he tries to escape, he is swallowed by a monster of a fish. Jonah himself is a sport, a mutation. A prophet who modestly protests is seemly; a prophet who balks altogether is a monster. "I prefer not to." What ails this Bartleby-prophet? God here is an amiable employer like Bartleby's, a good-natured, Pickwickian fellow who cajoles Jonah, tries to get him to see things reasonably. But no, Jonah prefers not to—against all odds. It will end badly for Jonah, as it ends for Melville's Bartleby. Jonah will go down, as Bartleby went down.

Down, down, down, goes Jonah. Down to Tarshish, instead of Nineveh. Down to the sea in a ship. Down into the sea itself, thrown overboard. Down into the belly of the monster fish. Then farther down, to the bottom of the sea, to the bottom of despair, where the weeds wrap themselves around his head.

And we, too, fall on Yom Kippur, in the late afternoon, when hunger and weariness weight us—down, down, to the bottom of the seas of the soul. There we encounter Jonah, who has a problem. What is his problem? He is so convinced God will show mercy to sinners, and the moral world will therefore go to rack and ruin, that he wants no part of the transaction, this Yom Kippur Jonah. Unlike the rest of his kind, prophets who plead with God for mercy even while they're warning the people they deserve none—"O Lord God, forgive, I beseech thee," cries Amos, "by whom shall Jacob arise? for he is small"—Jonah prefers to see, in this case, punishment instead. But though the vine under which he is sheltered is destroyed, the city itself is saved.

God then admonishes an angry Jonah, whose problem all along has been his faith in God's mercy, to have more faith in God's mercy.

"I know you are a gracious God . . . and slow to anger," Jonah says. Yet what is swifter than the anger of God? Think of what happened to the worshippers of the golden calf, to Sodom and

Gomorrah, and how Abraham had to plead for the release of fifty just men, of twenty, of ten. Abraham Heschel, in his book on the prophets, *stresses* God's anger, in fact, calls it the passion of the Lord's wrath, and finds in it evidence of the warmth with which God confronts His creation. "It is because . . . [God] cares for man that his anger may be kindled against man." Dispassionate punishment—uncaring, detached—is what the *pagan* gods meted out.

Jonah, too, is passionate. If he falls asleep on the ship in the midst of the storm, it's far from indifference. Nothing makes for sleep like depression. Jonah's turning away is full of anger. He's not destroying the relationship between God and prophet with coldness, but angrily, passionately naysaying. No!

Why, then, on a day when Jews beg for God's mercy, should a recalcitrant, disobedient Jew like Jonah be thrust into the forefront of God's consciousness?

The Book of Jonah is meant to teach Jews the power of repentance to earn God's mercy, and to remind them to be merciful. Isn't it also a reminder to God? You, who showed unstinting mercy to the pagan, show it also to us, who do know our right hand from our left but keep getting them mixed up anyway. All of Yom Kippur begs God to forgive. The story of Jonah, in which God chides Jonah into remembering mercy, on Yom Kippur is the very one we cast at the feet of God to stay the death-dealing hand, to stir up a memory of mercy. Nineveh had only 120,000 souls; on Yom Kippur we think of Europe's eleven million who perished in the Holocaust, six million of them Jews, one-third of their number in the world, cut off from the pity of Nineveh.

As for Jonah, whether Nineveh does or doesn't merit mercy is in the end no longer the point. Jonah is dissatisfied with all the endings. He'd rather—in his horrifying hubris—shape his own. How like a writer Jonah is. Between polar opposites, the tightrope is strung. In the tension between the rage to call down judgment on evildoing and the longing for mercy bestowed is the place, the prayer, out of which the writer writes.

Ah, Jonah! Ah, humanity!

—1987

Minority Writers and the Mainstream: Telling Stories in the Houses We Create

During a New England stay I visited writers' houses—Emerson's and Hawthorne's Old Manse at Concord, the site of Thoreau's shack at Walden Pond—and from the street beyond the garden (having arrived on the wrong day) sent a longing eye through what I hoped was the window of Emily Dickinson's room in her father's house at Amherst. Stripped of the messy heat of living, such houses acquire museum formality; they become the docent's domain. Once they belonged to writers who quarreled with society or were separated from it in their own time; now they are treasures of our mainstream.

I thought of these writers and their houses recently when asked by the woman's college I attended to take part in a "celebration of women reading and writing." The epigraph of my panel was "This Unkind House," with a text from the black playwright, Lorraine Hansberry, who died in 1965: "O, the things that we have learned in this unkind house that we have to tell the world about!" Unofficially, the panel's title was "Minority Writers and the Mainstream."

My copanelists were two black writers who, together with an Hispanic writer serving as moderator, called themselves collectively "women of color." This made me, a Jew and not a woman of color, a minority in this panel on minority writers. Possibly each of the other writers present also felt like a minority of one in some way.

I was not happy about the invitation. The truth is, I have never thought of myself as a minority writer. Every minority writer was first a minority person, but it's easier to accept minority status in life than in it is in art. The former is what you're supposed to transcend in the latter. Applied to life, "minority" is a statement

97

about demographics; when it leaks into literature it carries traces of elements less benign. Saul Bellow and Toni Morrison are both members of minority populations in the eyes of demographers, yet no one but an anthologist desperate for textbook adoption would dream of calling them minority writers.

Still, the truth about writers is that they all come from somewhere. The smallest of hometowns, the maternal womb, is always located in a particular time, place, and person. If your college, seizing upon your facts, translates all that complexity to minority status, what else can you do but bow to their view of things at least this once? I was admitted to Mount Holyoke under the quota for Jewish students. What was it, exactly? Two percent? No one quite cares to say. I understand that practices were no different at other Ivy League or Seven Sisters Colleges in those closing days of World War II. I am only sketching a little picture of what some of our houses were like in those days.

All of us were compelled to attend morning chapels, some of them religious. I was not uncomfortable with that. On the contrary, it was really there, listening half awake to hymns sung by the Glee Club, that I first realized how deep a vein of religious feeling ran in me. My first-generation Jewish parents had eliminated most religious observance from our lives in response to their time and place as they interpreted them. For me the point of this now is that all of it—quota, Christian observance for students of a different religion (though we were few)—was going on in the benign atmosphere of a high-minded woman's college, among the clean and beautiful hills of the Connecticut Valley, at the very time that one-third of the Jews of the world were being dragged off to the killing camps.

There came into the faculty one year a small Frenchman, a frail and trembly man, to teach philosophy. We knew his story, or thought we did. He had escaped from a concentration camp and mysteriously arrived at our campus. He had been starved and he ate voraciously, though he could not put on weight. He was charming. He said, "Ze 'th' zey nevair bozzer me."

Jean Wahl was a poet, an existential philosopher, and an absent-minded professor whose shoelaces were always untied. In some distant, abstract way we knew that he had suffered, but we were able to nudge him into some conception of normalcy. We laughed at him affectionately of course. He was the good-natured stranger who had come under our roof, and we were the undergraduates who knew—nothing at all.

I translated lines of M. Wahl's poetry:

Ah! how empty and vast and beautiful this world is,
Such loveliness scattered among the ruins. . . .

And still I did not understand. In the 1960s I tried to teach myself something by writing a novel called *Touching Evil,* to discover in the shadow of concentration camps the commentary on my own innocently sunlit life. I invented a student at a woman's college very much like mine who wakes from her peaceful bucolic slumber in the peaceful wartime campus when she sees the photographs of corpses in the camps liberated by the U.S. Army. There are no Jews in the book except the ones who are dead. The living characters are members of the minority of those who know, who are conscious, who connect.

At the International PEN (Poets, Essayists, Novelists) Congress in New York some winters ago, Toni Morrison, who had already won a Pulitzer prize for one of her novels, said that she had never felt like an American, though she had tried all her life to be one. As for me, I felt most like an American when I felt least like myself: when I was wrapped in the aura of a White Anglo-Saxon Protestant college campus that was my temporary home during four serene college years that happened to coincide with the nadir of human history.

None of us on the panel, as it turned out, was quite sure what house Lorainne Hansberry had in mind when she wrote that sentence. Was the unkind house her country? Or the families people live in, like the characters in her play, *A Raisin in the Sun?* Did she mean any of the other possible housings of the spirit? Could she, by any chance, have meant herself, or a combination of all these things?

A hundred or so years ago, during what is now called the American Renaissance, writers like Melville, Emerson, and Whitman wrote of their triumphant at-homeness in America, free at last of cultural dependence on Europe. Those illustrious early students of the American experience—Emerson, Hawthorne, Melville, Thoreau, Margaret Fuller—were concerned with how they could express what the country had to teach them. They had no American models, they *were* the models: their power came from originating. Some of the infighting among university professors now is not about the power of originating but about power conferred by models, and number of models. (How many battalions do you have in the Literary Canon?) In its most mindless aspect, canon-revision is aimed simply at overthrow. At its gentlest, this view expresses concern for minority students. Broaden the literary offerings studied in college classes, give students models to hook their own life experiences to, give them, the saying goes, a stake in the culture: bring in work of minorities, ethnics, races, religions, regardless of intrinsic worth (itself, in the minds of radical overthrowers, a devalued concept). Does this mean that Americans must be like those blind men feeling the elephant? Will we all identify only our part of the tail or the trunk or the mammoth legs or the floppy ears?

All this makes too complex an issue to be answered with anecdote. But I can't resist reporting on my observation of how the supposed beneficiaries of reformist goodwill want sometimes to discount its claims. For several years I was a teacher of evening classes made up mostly of minority, poverty-level women over forty. We had been comparing John Dewey's humane, experiential approach in education to the unrelenting regimen imposed on John Stuart Mill by his father, who stuffed his son with classical Greek and other mental strenuosities from age three on, without letup or leisure for reflection, imagination, or choice. To this source Mill himself traced the origins of his nervous breakdown—comfort enough, I thought, for education-deprived students. I was easing them toward Dewey's praise of experience (they'd had plenty of that), but they shot out ahead of me. Opting for discipline, authority, and early flowering, these life-burdened women lifted their heads above those late-night desks and cried with one voice, "I wish I'd had a father who made me do that!"

In my own case it would have helped if in my college years at the close of World War II some academic worth had been attached to the culture that was being snuffed out; if the curriculum could have included—if not in the canon then at least in some mention— the flowering of Jewish writers. Henry James knew about them (he commented on their power and worried that their excesses would pollute English). William Dean Howells helped to introduce Abraham Cahan to readers of *The Atlantic,* and Mark Twain referred to himself as the American Sholom Aleichem. Anzia Yezierska, the Polish-Jewish immigrant writer, had already been taken up by literary critics and afterwards had fallen into obscurity. Although sparsely translated, there were first-rate Yiddish poets and thinkers. Why were students, in that time and place, kept ignorant of them? When Anzia Yezierska and the American philosopher, John Dewey, became lovers—astonishingly, secretly, and against all odds—weren't they, whatever else they were doing, making incarnate for a little while the attraction/repulsion of mutual longing, the love duet of minority and mainstream?

If we start from another point on the periphery of argument, we encounter Edmund Wilson's suggestion in "The Wound and the Bow" that writers are like Philoctetes, whose festering wound so repels us that he must be banished, yet whose magical gifts we require for survival. Writers are outsiders; they make up their own minority. Isaac Rosenfeld, in *An Age of Enormity,* says this about minority status: "Since modern life is so complex that no man [I think he meant "or woman"] can possess it in its entirety, the outsider often finds himself the perfect insider." The second part of his idea is as wise as the first, but less frequently quoted. He resists overvaluing alienation: "It is undesirable, for it falls short of the full human range."

No writer sets out to enrich the mainstream. Writers begin smaller, closer to home, sifting through self to grasp the world. Country, college, family—they all house us. But most intimately and antagonistically, I house myself. The unkindest house may in the end be the self-tormenting mind, the beast in the jungle at home. What one most struggles for is an *inner* room of one's own, encountering-place for recognitions. Sometimes inner and outer rooms coincide. In offering up themselves, writers also bear witness to the follies of the society that won't admit them. The uncongenial isolated personage of Emily and Charlotte Bronte's childhood is reflected in the houses they created in their writings— Emily in *Wuthering Heights:* gloomy, cold, empty of love, and filled with destructive passion; Charlotte in *Jane Eyre.* Her aptly named Thornfield, with its madwoman in the attic, is distorted into gothic horror by the ego of Mr. Rochester, who will later be tamed, controlled, made to fit inside a house hacked down, like him, from grandiosity to something that can begin to approach human scale. These female writers who had to disguise authorship under masculine names are now part of England's and English literature's cherished mainstream.

Despite Virginia Woolf's tragic view, her death-drenched awareness, her madness, her eventual suicide, she was—whoever reads her diaries must be struck full in the face by this—a *happy* woman, centered in the life of her time. One of the greatest expressions of her joy is in houses. Think of the one in *To the Lighthouse,* sandy, windy, crammed with children and friends, open to the sea and steadied like a great ship by Mrs. Ramsey herself, the mother and master of these lives. Virginia Woolf confided her fear to her diaries that bouts of madness would be detected in her writing and pull it askew. But who is more mainstream to us today than Virginia Woolf?

No house it seems to me was ever kinder to a writing woman than was Jane Austen's family house, Chawton Cottage. In it she was honored, supported, loved, listened to, enjoyed. So what if she had to slip pages under her embroidery hoop when someone entered the room? Under that quaint cover, she sat intimate among the ducks like a hunter in her blind, and from that snug space created an architecture of such large and generous proportions that within it mansions could rise. She taught life's human lessons (it is the reason writers write) in those great houses that sprang from her pen, stone on stone: Northanger Abbey, Netherfield, Rosings, Pemberly Hall, Mansfield Park. Secure in her judgments, unerring in her fictional maneuverings, outspoken about all social arrangements, marital and financial. Though a woman and therefore, one might have thought, marginal to the worldly business of the eighteenth century, she reflects the very center of her age.

Webster's *New Twentieth Century Dictionary* definition of minority says it is "A racial, religious, national, or political group smaller than and differing from the larger, controlling group of which it is a part." When we speak of minorities do we mean literal minorities in the sense of belonging to a group small in number, or metaphorical minority in the sense of people whose literary voice has not yet been heard? Maybe it's really immigrants of one sort or another we are talking about, after all. No doubt there is something off to one side, not mainstream, in *their* work.

The newly arrived, to the land or to literature, are apt to behave bizarrely. Civilities sink beneath the struggle to survive. Sex and/or violence may be flagrant. New rhythms rough things up. Yet Thomas Wentworth Higginson said that Emily Dickinson's poems seemed torn up by the roots with earth still clinging to them. Should we then include Dickinson among minorities of a separate category based on oddness and unacceptability in one's time (Dickinson was, Edith Wharton wasn't)?

The critic Philip Rahv, in words that may now seem to us naive, divided writing into rough, emotive "redskin" as opposed to smoother "paleface" literature. In England, Bloomsbury, having thought itself so shocking, was itself shocked when the voice of D. H. Lawrence, so immediate and raw and redskin, broke into the smooth flow of British diction. In America, the country celebrated by Whitman's "barbaric yawp," critics have been less resistant to stretching literature to include its newcomers. Yet Henry James worried about English being under assault from hungry hearts (the phrase is Anzia Yezierska's) that wanted to bend English to their needs. Whatever the dimensions of the dialogue, our literature along with our population continues to change in ways utterly unforeseen.

Do we assume that the dominant voice in American letters has been male? The American Renaissance writers do seem to have been a crowd of men (though by no means a coherent group: Hawthorne despised Emerson, Melville adored Hawthorne who was bent on escaping him, Thoreau had his doubts about almost everybody else, and so on). But poor lone Margaret Fuller, no more eccentric than her Concord peers, or less gifted a haranguer, was condescended to as the one dancing dog among them. Not until her ship literally sank and she drowned in the sea could she win their grudging acclaim.

Yet American voices have often been the voices of eccentrics and loners—minority, if you like. The outsider, we remember, is one definition of the artist. What was mainstream about Haw-thorne, a weaver of moonbeamy romances about good and evil? Or about Thoreau, a misfit who did what writers always do when they make mythology out of personal pain? What, come to think of it, is so mainstream about our Nobel Prize winners in literature? Established in 1901, the prize was copped by French, German,

Spanish, Italian, and British writers until 1930, when an American writer was finally found fit to win: Sinclair Lewis, midwest muckraker. In 1936 it was Eugene O'Neil writing of dark-fated Irish-American families afflicted with addictions; in 1938 Pearl Buck, writing of China; in 1949 William Faulkner, psalmist of the Lost Cause of the South; followed five years later by Hemingway, mourner of lost masculine innocence; and in eight more years John Steinbeck, who seemed a locale-revised version of winner number one. After that nobody till two Jews—Saul Bellow in 1976 and I. B. Singer in 1978. Milosz, who won in 1980, was formed in Poland, and Brodsky, who won in 1987, in the USSR. Outsiders all, one might say. Minorities.

If minority is "a group within a country . . . that differs in race, religion, or national origin from the dominant group," what on earth is our dominant group? WASPS? In that case, is their literary spokesman Louis Auchincloss, and is that our dominant voice? Hardly. Two women, Edith Wharton and Willa Cather, with large endowed inherited holdings in the American scene and landscape, have each created a dominant literature. Yet they have produced utterly different voices. America's literary pluralism seems built into its geography.

Which of America's voices now being heard—male or female, mainstream (whatever that is) or minority (ditto)—will connect with that kind of centrality? The outcome, unknown to us here, will be revealed in the house of our future. There remains that matter of the desired full human range.

—1989

Notes Toward a Holocaust Fiction

1. THE BOY IN THE PHOTOGRAPH

Having completed a story,* I feel puzzled. The story is a fiction based on truth (though with altered characters and point of view), an almost-memoir about the way something happened: a trip to Vienna with my husband, who was born there. With or without these fictional changes, the story asks the one question I believe worth asking: How, after the Holocaust, can we live now?

Why did I want to write a fictionalized account instead of a memoir? Perhaps to give distance; maybe to give some hope. Also to be truer: left alone, reality can't be trusted to convey itself.

I can't dictate to others, but for myself, I never want to invent Holocaust scenes. In fact I have a horror of it, as of something that might add to the sum of pain. And this despite my knowing that in Holocaust fiction there can be no invention of event. Whatever can be imagined has happened. The Holocaust transformed to reality what should have occurred only in nightmares.

I do not want to invent Holocaust scenes. Maybe that was why, now, I wanted to write real Holocaust scenes as fiction.

Maybe this, maybe that. The truth is I don't know why.

Somewhere in a Bellow novel a character tries to get another character to shape up: "Your father had rich blood in his veins, he sold apples." Our fathers and mothers had rich blood in their veins and it was spilled and spilled. Whether or not we're crazy with the weight and grief of it, we are astonishingly sane. Only sanity remembers. Sanity makes a home for the dead.

This raises a terrifying question: How are we to create anew, how go forward into life at all, if we are so weighted with memory?

There is no beginning and no end to thinking about the Holocaust. We spend our lives reading witness books, looking at

---

* "The Cheek of the Trout," *Testimony,* Harcourt, Brace, Jovanovitch, 1990.

films of testimony, and we know nothing. Behind every degradation, every terror published or recounted, horrors we cannot know
lie buried with those who could not survive. The worst of sadistic
fantasy? Decency once warned us to push it down. Allow it free
rein now. What is your most bestial imagining? No, more than
that. Worse. Given power by actuality. Caring for a child, reading
Wordsworth with students, comforting a sick friend, we are all
caught forever, at the bottom of the mind's mud, in mockery of
love. These things have been. And quite, quite recently, polluting
the human psyche forever.

My story asks the question: How can we live now?

Not long ago the poet Czeslaw Milosz published a letter in *The
New York Review of Books* defending himself against a *favorable*
review of his work. What upset him was that he had been characterized as a witness, "which for him [the reviewer] is perhaps a
praise, but for me is not." Milosz went on: "An insane course of
history tore out of me during the war anti-Nazi poems of anger
and solidarity with the victims. And yet we should distinguish
between our duty to preserve memory and our natural desire to
move forward with our affairs of the living. People should not
freeze, magnetized by the sight of evil perpetrated in our lifetime."
The poet then goes on to speak of "the dynamics at the very core of
any art: ". . . a poet repeatedly says farewell to his old selves and
makes himself ready for renewals."

Compare this with another statement. It is from Primo Levi's
The Drowned and the Saved. "Anyone who has been tortured
remains tortured."

Milosz's wisdom is akin to nature's wisdom: death and re-
newal. We say easily enough that the Holocaust is the central
occurrence of the twentieth century, but we act sometimes as if we
don't believe it. We slide out from under its weight now and then
or we can't live as artists or as human beings, either. If we allow the
full weight, what then? A literature of apocalypse—dark, satanic,
black with wretchedness and grieving. If we wish to go on writing
about lovers and children and trust and hope and families and
springtime, we suppress knowledge of the Holocaust, relieved to
be, now and then, inauthentic beings who hide from ourselves
what we know. *Henderson the Rain King* is Saul Bellow's vacation
from the Holocaust. Creating a gentile Henderson (or at least

proclaiming him so) with no duty to preserve memory was one means of sending a character out into the world in free search of adventure. Jewish writers take such working vacations, creating an "as if" world. As if it never happened.

I have written my share of "as if" pieces. I have also published essays with such titles as "The Holocaust and the American-Jewish Novelist," "A Second Life of Holocaust Imagery," as well as a whole series of short stories that spring from a different "as if"— as if we were never free to stop thinking of the Holocaust. In my novel, *Touching Evil*, American non-Jews respond to their first knowledge of the Holocaust by asking themselves, "How can we live now?" Non-Jews, says that book, suffer from Holocaust knowledge, too. This is what human beings could do, and did. It was the peculiar genius of the Jew to fetch it forth, but the malaise, the malediction of that knowledge has entered the psyche of Jew and non-Jew alike.

I wanted to call my novel *Heart's Witness,* or *Witness Through Imagination.* My "as if" world is as if no one can escape the knowledge. One character encounters it as an undergraduate in the forties. A teacher, in despair at his own discovery, makes a sexual conquest of her: seduction through concentration camp pictures, initiation into the facts of grown-up life. For her, thereafter, the symbolic figure is the woman who claws her way up from the bottom of a pile of corpses, barely buried, the earth spouting blood at that spot. A woman of the next generation, pregnant and watching the Eichmann trial televised in the early sixties, with its testimony of surviving victims, is overcome by terror, the child in her womb menaced by what has been loosed in the world. For her the symbolic figure is the pregnant woman in the death camp, laboring on lice-infested straw, giving birth at the booted feet of a guard.

I too was pregnant in 1961, watching the Eichmann trial every day through the promising spring and the suffocating heat of summer, asking the question: How can we live now?

How we first encountered the Holocaust and how we reencounter it over and over—these are the touchstones of our time. A very old Japanese painter once said, near the end of his life, "I am just learning to draw a straight line." If I live a long life, I, too, will say, "I am just learning to draw a line from myself to the Holocaust."

When I wrote of the devastation in the woman who makes her discovery at the time the camps were opened and photographs were released, I believed it was invention. Later, I read Susan Sontag's *On Photography* and found her description—"a negative epiphany"—of her first sight, at age twelve, of photographs from the camps in 1945:

> Nothing I have seen—in photographs or in real life—ever cut me as sharply, deeply, instantaneously. Indeed, it seems plausible to me to divide my life into two parts, before I saw those photographs . . . and after, though it was several years before I understood fully what they were about. . . . When I looked at those photographs, something broke. Some limit had been reached, and not only that of horror; I felt irrevocably grieved, wounded, but a part of my feelings started to tighten; something went dead; something is still crying.

When I started I didn't know about that. Between 1961 and 1962, when I was reading and taking notes in preparation for writing the book completed in 1967, little in the way of the subject's present astonishing bibliographical richness had surfaced. But I was not doing research. I was stumbling upon books—memoirs, diaries, factual accounts like dirges—*The Black Book of Poland*—and recoiling, then making myself go back and read on. Those texts, and the televised recollections of witnesses at the Eichmann trial (supplemented daily in the *Herald Tribune* far more fully, I seem to recall, than in *The New York Times*), were enough to start the landslide of images that were to become my novel. A sliver of any one of them would have been sufficient.

Most of all I listened to my husband's accounts of his childhood in Vienna before he left on a children's transport a few weeks after Kristallnacht. The Jewish *Kultesgemeinde* managed to save his life, but not the lives of his father and mother or of a large extended family. More than four decades later we went to Vienna, that flower-planted city, and saw it in inverse relation to its perfection: the shadow that lies beneath, the past within the present.

Ordinary pleasures and, I suppose, in Nadezhda Mandelstam's phrase, "ordinary heartbreak," which we try to encompass in our post-Holocaust era in order to create life out of survival, are in some way forever beyond us. The delicacy of a sweetmeat, a delectable food that completely fills and satisfies, cannot fill and satisfy us because we are already filled with our history. Even if we wish to forget the past, so simple a thing as a fork knocking against a fish bone may remind us.

People in my story dine on trout. The fish known as trout is also "The Trout," the Schubert quintet of melting beauty, *Die Forelle*. What do we think of beautiful German music? Do we think or do our nerves react for us? Concentration camp commandants were often men of "culture" who would finish the day's hideous work and then repair to an evening of beautiful German music. In Auschwitz the S.S. commandant kept a quartet of gifted prisoners playing German music day and night as Jews stumbled to the gas chambers.

I once heard an innovative cantor lead the singing of *Adon Olam*, God of the world, to the "Ode to Joy" theme of the last movement of Beethoven's *Ninth*. No one was entirely happy, but no one thought it right not to be happy, either. "What is it? What do you want from a melody? What is a melody anyway? Besides, it predates all that. And when did Jews have melodies of their own . . . ?" The beautiful can't be enjoyed unless the moral component is evaluated, and that makes life a burden, but when was a life unburdened by moral component ever worth living?

And yet—when is memory an act of homage, and when does it hold us hostage? Buildings, monuments, national and personal relations bridge themselves over the past. Repair, repair, says the world. The act of memory is an affront to life, which reseeds each season. Jews affront life, with their eternal remembering: life affronts Jews, with its eternal obliterating.*

---

* I have argued with a friend, D., about the images in a film whose story was written by the German writer Peter Handke, in collaboration with the moviemaker Wim Wenders and called in English *Wings of Desire:* concentration camp inmates, SS guards (even if they appear only in a movie within the movie), bombed-out German cities in World War II, and young Germans wandering about in a general air of malaise and confusion. Mystical German angels float in the air, listening impassively to the inner anguish of the populace, and then moving on in what seemed to me an inadvertent parody of the German people themselves who could hear, and not hear, the anguish of Jewish neighbors forty years before.

D. argued that Germans and Austrians are victims of their history and, like

On and on it goes, this argument with ourselves. When we commit to our pastimes—when we eat, make love, reproduce, create shapes of language on paper—each stroke of joy casts up a dark echo. That is my story, or rather, it is mine to the degree that it is not mine alone.

When I was about twelve, the age of Susan Sontag when the photographs of Dachau and Bergen-Belsen produced her "negative epiphany," I also saw a photo. My parents were sent a picture from Germany of a boy of about the same number of years as I. He was stocky, with round, smiling cheeks; he wore knickers, and his arms hung awkwardly by his side. His parents, who were distant relatives of my father's, were pleading for us to send an affidavit so the boy could escape Hitler.

My mother grieved that it was not a girl, and said she would gladly have sent for her to share my room. But without an extra bedroom, where could a robust boy like that be accommodated?

The photograph was put away somewhere. The boy no doubt died somewhere else. The rest of us went on in some very different fashion, although it is true that I am married to man who escaped from Austria at about the age of the boy in the photograph.

2. THE CHEEK OF THE TROUT

"Enjoy the city for me," he kept saying, as if he *counted* on the difference between them. He had lived there and she had not, he was European and she American, he steeped in politics and she in art history, on the lookout for the interesting and beautiful. They

---

all victims of catastrophe, can't allow themselves to remember. He likes it that these two German artists aren't trying to say too much, that they admit impotence and inability to make meaning of their own and their nation's history. It is an anti-meaning film, says D., because, after all that happened, they do not trust meaning, they have limited ambitions, which D. approves in art. He prefers this confession of impotence, this anti-heroic admission of damage.

For me such Holocaust aesthetics don't exist. Concentration camp prisoners in their striped uniforms, bunks from which those haunted eyes peered out, booted SS guards—these images strike upon the synapses so violently that they skew the weights and balances of things, they tip and sink other cargo like a capsized *Titanic*. For me Holocaust images cannot be some among many. Writers have the responsibility to avoid resisting meaning with all their strength.

were the same age, but on this trip she felt younger than her husband. He kept trying to explain something and then stopping, as if he thought it was hopeless, she could never understand. She almost agreed. His explanations seemed to be falling into some part of her that was missing.

This didn't happen so much when they were going around the official part of the city: he had not lived his boyhood there. But when they walked into the old, outer districts, he would now and then stop in his tracks. She found herself stopping too, and when he stared at a house or a corner of a street on which there was nothing, she also stared, and her heart began to pound.

Once, stopping, he said, "My uncle's store was there, someone must have stepped right in, right away, afterward. Look, it's still going strong, which neighbor could it have been?" And he stood trying to imagine which one, but making no move toward the place.

As they walked away she said—like a fool, but it was out of tenderness for what he had said, and tact, a certain kind of tact that knew he required her not to speak directly or with pity for any of this—that she loved the old-fashioned wood dividers of the front windows. He nodded, he acknowledged what she said, but had no reply to it then. Later, in another place, he said, "Here's a carved door for you!" pleased to have found it for her.

In the formal part of the city things were easier. "Be a tourist," he said. "Look at everything and enjoy it, otherwise it's not fair to yourself."

Sometimes she complained, "You think I don't know anything about life because, compared to this, I've only been happy." It was her happiness grumbling. She accepted her role. The beauty of the city was making her drunk, in spite of what she knew—of course she knew it! And to be there with her husband, who had at his fingertips history and politics and languages and art, too, though he lingered least on that, felt to her like the supremest security.

He relied on her too, of course, to see the beauty of the place where he had been born, leaving him free to be as blind to it as he needed to be on this first return after four decades. Had she expected to see bridges sag? Facades pockmarked by corruption as if they were paintings by the Albrecht twins? As if a place could be punished like the picture of Dorian Gray? She reported to him, as if he were blind: Now there is beauty, wholeness, prosperity, repair. Buildings bore fine stone sculpture, even the ones without special plaques. On rooftops, life-sized stone figures offered books, instruments of music and science, to the populace below. She turned her gaze up to them, drinking in their gifts. Doing her job, she described them, she snapped their pictures with her camera.

When they needed directions, he did the asking, caught for a moment with strangers in the intimacy of mother tongue. His manner with people seemed perfect—his dignity, his self-control. He was stocky, handsome, gray-haired. She would watch him approach each one, guessing at whether they guessed why he was a stranger now, though in command of their dialect. Nothing was betrayed on either side—polite, polite.

When people in the street seemed about the right age she asked, "Can any of these possibly be the same as the ones who were here then?" And to show how much she knew—of course she knew!—"I mean the neighbors who put on their swastika buttons right after Hitler marched in—you told me they did that—as if they'd already worn them hidden under their coats?" Then, her voice rising in a kind of anxious demand that he acknowledge that she knew: "The ones who attacked your father? Who slapped you in the street one day, a child on your way to school?" Her voice broke on that, ample warning, if she needed it, that this was the wrong tone. She stopped at once.

In silence they stood before the doorway of the house where he had lived; in silence followed his path to school through the tree-shaded alleys of the *Augarten,* a park so clean and neatly planted she might never have believed in its existence; in silence sat on a bench beside the broad road called the *Hauptallee,* where his parents rested in the open air on Sundays and his little-boy self, untouched by sadness then, played with friends. When the bench sent forth too many emanations, he got up and walked rapidly away. She shot after him, catching at his hand. He fumbled with the other across both their chests, not looking, to give the side of her hair a quick caress—he reassuring *her!*

From the beginning they knew the trip would be too painful. From the beginning it was too full of silences between them. She filled them in for herself. She imagined they were not who they were, a couple approaching this pain from their own chronology, one of them having had the worst experience it is possible to have, and now for the first time going back. She invented: We are a young man and young woman, his name is Joshua, hers is— whatever—Joan, it's better to be young here, we're intimate with each other but in a different way, we have empathy for the past, but with veils of distance, we'd each have parents, but it's Joshua's father who's the Holocaust survivor, his pain wouldn't so immediately be ours. She imagined this as much for her husband as herself, wanting him to have some refuge.

She'd read of people, there are case histories about them, who under the assault of pain split off into other personalities. But she was fearful of what she was doing. How could she dare attempt such an alleviating gesture? After a while she developed little ironies about it. "Really? You're not just yanking away a few years? Not just preening yourself on giving comfort where there's none to be given?"

It came anyway—little waves of Joshua and Joan, invention making its own complications.

Joshua telephones his father and Joan hears him too in the echoing booth warning Joshua to keep this, keep that, afraid of more losses.

"Keep your dignity," his father says. "If you accidentally bump into someone, keep your head high. Keep your distance, you're an American, you're looking them over. Right now I'd like to pull you out of there but all right, you're another generation, you can keep separate, it's not the same for you."

Then Joan calls her mother and Joshua has to hear her tell Joan to give everything away. "You're holding back for Joshua's sake, and that's not right. There's not a thing in the world wrong with that city, it's the cleanest and safest of any in Europe, your father and I had a wonderful time when we were there, but you're not giving yourself to it. It's not Joshua, it's his father I blame, someone who can't allow people to give themselves to the present now where they're completely safe and well. . . ."

Joshua is small-boned, with curly brown hair, unbelievably watchful eyes, and now a new reddish mustache, started for their trip. Joan thinks: *their* trip, but it's Joshua's, it's Joshua's father's with Joshua making it for him. The complications of the invention grow. How, for example, did Joan meet Joshua? In an art history lecture at a university, the same as themselves? Yes, Joan made a beeline toward the vacant seat beside Joshua, toward the two expressions in his face, sadness and the wish to be happy. "Oh, I'll see you're happy," Joan is always thinking.

On the second day they went to the Jewish cemetery, they themselves, not Joshua and Joan. They searched for a gravestone arranged for from America. Her husband held a slip of paper with location, row and number, and a lone laborer encountered in the otherwise empty vastness, a Yugoslav worker, helped with hand signs. At last they found the place, swellings in the earth, neglected stones pushed crooked like teeth in an infected gum, but it was not from his parents, they were not buried anywhere, though her husband for this moment wanted to believe his father's ashes were here. Would they be? Would the bureaucrats of Buchenwald where his father died of typhus have ordered the ashes of individuals to be carefully scooped and labeled and sent home because it was still in the early years of killings, or had they shoveled and dumped the bushel-loads and picked names to call them? Did it matter whose ashes these were? Yes, for now, to her husband, it mattered, and mattered that his mother's could never be reclaimed. Where is Antigone in a world of human ashpits?

Late afternoon summer sun spilled over the ground and honeyed the leaves on the trees. In this prodigality of light, who would believe in darkness? She stood apart. Her husband began to speak a prayer before the writing on the stone. Mother and Father, names on a gravestone. When his voice broke into tight, fought-off sobs, she thought, Where are Joshua and Joan? But it was no use, it was themselves standing there. A little door opened in her husband's broad chest and a twelve-year-old tumbled out weeping. She opened her arms to catch him.

Leaving, they lost their way. The gravestones on this path were bigger, they had elaborate gothic lettering, titles. *Vizeburgermeister* and *Obermedizinalrat* and *Kaiserlicher Rat* and *Reichsratsabgeordneter*. "What's this, what's that?" she asked. "Heads of things," he answered. "Medical organizations, city councils." "Why are these so bare?" She meant the names beneath the ornamented ancestors. Then she noticed the dates, 1937 to 1945. There was luck even among the dead.

She could sound out these words herself. *Vergast Belsec, Ges-*

torben in Theresienstadt. Jews of the world, you know more German than you think. *Verschleppt nach Auschwitz. Umgekommen in Dachau. Ermordet in Belsen.* She copied words into her notebook, but not fast enough, and turned to snapping the camera. Sun glinted on granite, obliterating names, but she went on snapping till she couldn't anymore, and ran down the path, he after her.

Then they were back at the beginning, and entered a low room, cryptlike, filled with filing cabinets. Her husband spoke to a man reading behind a desk who rose, a long cotton coat of rusty black uncreasing itself down to his shoetops.

At first her husband translated for her. "This gentleman is the keeper of records here. He spent the Hitler years in Argentina." Then the man spoke to her in good English. "Enjoy this beautiful city." The man's smile was sweet. Not a melancholy smile, only slow. "It is your first time here, enjoy it."

She flinched a little at that, as usual. "And also go to the mountains," said the record-keeper, the cemetery man, like a sybil, like a good elf, "my mother's favorite place, ah, the wonderful air. In the mountains was always my mother's cure, you should go, enjoy everything."

An encouraging breath expanded inside her. She blurted, God knew why, knowing it was idiocy the moment she spoke, "Is she there now?" The record-keeper's smile slowly faded. He gave her a prolonged look, as if assessing how it might be possible to infuse intelligence into her at last.

On the trolley ride back to the hotel, silent again, she imagined the life of the cemetery man in Argentina. What was it? He had to learn Spanish. All right, that was no problem, she quickly arranged for him to do so. He had to learn to live. How? She pictured the little man in rusty black duster (take that off him, for God's sake, he's not wearing it in Argentina!) blundering with a prayer book under his arm among the gauchos and tango dancers. At first the fantasy diverted her. Then in winding streets it turned grim. Searching out a fellow Jew to speak German with, he encountered instead a fled Nazi prospering there. Mengele, who delighted in medical experiments, would ask if he had a twin, would fancy the special shape of those ironically slanted eyes, those drooping earlobes.

No—no, have him meet Borges, the great Argentinian writer!

"You yourself, dear man"—it's Borges speaking so kindly—"even without your old texts and Talmud-study companions, may dream commentaries. You yourself can write *A Guide to the Perplexed* by Maimonides." When the little fantasy was over she still saw the cemetery record-keeper in his long black coat, standing at the low window of his cryptlike room. Her husband stared through the window of the swaying trolley. A recorded voice announced street destinations in guttural German: *"Karl Lueger Strasse. . . ."*

For days after that they quieted themselves in the gilt-and-marble vaults of the Kunsthistorische Museum. Rembrandt, Brueghel, Bosch. . . . They followed a guide through the royal red-brocaded rooms of the Hofburg castle, stepping backward through history to the safe rococo Hapsburg monarchy. Hoop-la! The empress installed handrings in her apartment so she could turn somersaults.

Her husband said, "I feel the city's about to explode." But it was in themselves that the explosion came. One evening in a restaurant they encountered a couple from the States eating dinner at an adjacent table, the woman a small, neat body quietly consulting her guidebook, the man enormously fat and talky, his belly a Humpty Dumpty belted barrel. They had been, the man informed them from his table, on a whirlwind tour of highspots in the Slavic countries—Budapest, Prague, Dubrovnik, Warsaw.

"And what did I come for?" the man asked rhetorically, though they hadn't inquired. "I came to see a concentration camp." His little round eyes filled with tears, his voice choked off, he was unable to speak another word.

In their room that night she asked indignantly, "What right has he to cry like that? Why hasn't grief taken off a few pounds, why didn't he first lose weight if he was going to be a public mourner?" Her husband turned on her with a violence like the swing in a weather vane, like the stiff sudden movement of the medieval figures in the Hoher Markt Anker Clock.

"He has a right to his feelings no matter what he looks like!" Aesthetics had perverted her, he said in a fury, the city had done its work and seduced her with its beauty. "It's all you care about!"

"Then stop telling me to enjoy myself," she shouted back. "I'm not a tourist! How could I know you and not think of what went on here? I would think of it even if I didn't know you!"

What was horrible to them was that in this place he had fled as a child, had to be rescued from it before it hacked him to bits, they now hacked at one another. This was happening in their hotel room, itself a work of beauty, stuffed with darkly polished Biedermeier furniture, or at least with good enough imitations of it, its balcony overlooking the stone figures giving counsel to the populace below.

She had backed away from this outburst into the brass lock of the gleaming armoire and had hurt her elbow. He was pacing up and down the room in a rigid line while he circled his hand over his chest, like someone practicing a complicated coordination. She rubbed her arm, he circled with his palm what gripped in his chest. It was as if they were solving the riddle of where to locate pain. That was when they remembered the advice of the cemetery man, and wondered if it could save them.

"This reminds me—yes, the contrasts!—something like a Bosch"—in the mountains it was easier to recover the enthusiasm they both required of her—"or one of the Brueghels we saw, was that Salon Twelve or Thirteen?—never mind!" She would look it up later, but he knew what she meant. "At one side someone's painted a multitude climbing up, at the other side, what? All those people treading the downward path to the boiling lake?"

She had succeeded in making him laugh. He was relaxed now and wryly commenting. "So it's a level of hell after all?"

Enthusiasm always made her exaggerate, but there surely was this duality in the little mountain resort. The two important places were several miles apart. At one end of the village was the entrance to the mountain-climbing trails, at the other, a little beyond the center of the village, were the thermal pools. The place divided itself between the healthy and the sick.

"Everything's in twos!" she announced. "The city and the spa, the monument and the mountain, this generation, that generation. . . ." She let him know what she had been thinking about Joshua and Joan, too. He brushed his lips back and forth on her cheek—"Thanks for the mustache"—so they could both imagine the feel of it, bushy and red.

The dining room of their hotel was vast, but with only five tables set for breakfast. In the morning, among the scattered guests, they heard Italian, German, French. The waitress, a robust

young woman, greeted them in a cheery voice: *"Kaffee zweimal?"*
After she brought the two coffees and rolls she ran to the window
to watch her husband drive the crane that was dismantling the
hotel next door.

The proprietress was on crutches. Not, she assured them, from
a skiing accident, but only a stupid slip in her bathroom. Dressed
in sweater and skirt of matching loden green, she hung genteelly
between her props. "The young people nowadays prefer beaches in
the south of France. They have forgotten the mountains of their
parents." Not her voice, but the striking of her crutches on the
flagstones of the lobby, made the bitter sound.

The parents were out in full force. Handsome, hearty couples
in their silver-haired age strolled the streets. They wore sweaters
beautifully embroidered with edelweiss, knickers of moss-green
suede, knee socks of double-woven wool patterned in lozenge.
Their shoes were stout-soled brown leather, their alpine staffs ar-
mored with medallions: mountain goats and silver jugs and green
garlands edging the curved silver shields, emblems of Bad Gastein
and Salzburg and Bad-am-See.

One day her husband said, "An attendant gave me some information about this place. There are special baths here that contain a
form of radon. The sick ones come for the radon cure."

The absurdity seemed to fit in perfectly—soaring beauty
above, deadly emanations from below. Radon treatment was offered in the special baths as well as in the various inhalings and
absorptions from the gold mines deep underground. The brochures showed men and women lying on cots in full nakedness,
with lifted relaxed knees exposing the shadowed entrance between
the thighs, or the winesac of the scrotum and its soft spout.

The proprietress, confronted on her crutches, said forthrightly,
"Sure, before this, people came and sat for hours in the baths or
baked in the mines, then they went home and got sick! Now they
know better. They must consult a doctor here, who will regulate
everything."

One afternoon they sat at a table of an open-air restaurant at
the foot of the mountain, sipping coffee and breathing in the thin,
delicious air. They watched the climbers in their suedes and lodens,
as frozen in time as if the hands of the clock had never moved. She

saw from her husband's face what was the matter, and didn't need to ask. They were all about the right age.

They decided then to consort with the sick. It was there, among those wanting to be healed in the warm bubbly water, that they began to encounter other Jews. Before they left home, she had bought a tiny gold Shield of David on a chain to wear around her neck. All sorts of Jews swam up to them because of her star, she believed. All of them expressed preference for people of a different part of the world.

A Rumanian couple, widely traveled, said they could stomach all nationalities except Poles: "Terrible, terrible anti-Semites." "Personally we were made to feel comfortable when we visited Poland," said another couple from Europe. There were those who would not "set foot in Germany" and those who made a point of it. No matter which country was mentioned, someone was sure to say, "Others were as bad or worse." "And where we are this minute, Austria, do you want to start on that? We have to show that we are again a part of the universe."

These Jews, some younger, some older, seemed to be struggling to regain a kind of global poise. What attitude should they take toward the world? "This generation," they said, "is not that generation; this decade is not the one of forty years ago."

An Israeli couple swam over. They were leaving soon for Munich. They reported that Germans, Austrians, and Poles had been personally very nice to them when they visited there. "Israel is a small country, you have to travel."

Outside the pool they met a bearded Belgian Jew of about fifty who walked with a hip-hiking limp. He was married to a German woman in her twenties with piercing blue eyes, buck teeth, and a frank manner. The Belgian had a way of not speaking until he had taken one or both of them by the arm and moved a little ways off from where they had been standing: he could only be understood on fresh ground. He spoke in a confidential manner, even his jokes imparted directly into the ear like state secrets. He had one about the countries of Europe where Jews lived before Hitler: "They only killed you there"—he smiled and whispered—"you could live with it."

One day he drew both of them to one side, though not so far

that his wife couldn't hear. "She is a better Jew than I am," he said, dipping his head toward his wife. She approached, laughing. "What he means is that when we married, I tried to wake him early so he could attend Saturday services, but always he went back to sleep."

At night in their room they compared notes about the people they met. She wanted to say that the Belgian was too intimate about trivialities, too public about what should be private. But she remembered how they had quarreled over the fat man's tears and kept it to herself.

One day she sat the edge of the pool, waiting for her husband to finish his swim, when a female voice beside her said, "Too much illness and bad legs, how will I stand it here!" She turned to see an attractive young woman in a red bikini, beating up small waves in the water with her feet. "Still, if it helps Heinrich, I will certainly stay."

At that moment her husband emerged from the pool in the company of a man. "There he is," the young woman said, "there's Heinrich!" "And that's my husband." "So we have all become acquainted at the same time." The woman stuck out her hand with a smile. "Elsa. From Germany."

Elsa and Heinrich were both in their early thirties, an attractive couple. Heinrich looked struck by sunlight—even his eyebrows and lashes were blond. But he was melancholy. "I am supposed to be young, but this knee doesn't know it. After one little skiing accident, it refuses to heal properly and becomes arthritic."

"Heinrich is bored," Elsa announced.

"This literary conversation in the pool with your husband," Heinrich said, "is the first interest that has penetrated my life here."

"Heinrich is depressed. And we will have two more weeks of this." Elsa was laughing.

"Shall we meet for dinner tonight?" Heinrich asked in his drawling yet somehow excited English, "if we are not too boring and depressing for you? There is a restaurant called The Trout that serves fresh fish. A rarity in the mountains, yes?"

"What do you think of the young couple?" she called through the bathroom door while her husband showered. After glancing briefly at her, he had agreed to dinner in the most matter-of-fact way. His answer came muffled, but when he emerged, his naked body ruddy from its toweling, he looked directly at her and asked, "Did you feel we shouldn't go?"

In the shower, water drumming on her head, she'd heard an echo of *Heinrich's* father this time, telephoning his son with homilies from Hamburg: "If you meet any Jews, don't hang your head. It's true your grandfather joined the Nazi party for business reasons, and I became an S.S. officer when I was young, but whatever we did you're another generation, you had nothing to do with it, you don't owe an apology. If you meet a Jew, you can be friendly, offer a glass of wine if you can stand to be with them, but on no account are you required to apologize."

Her head was becoming like the thermal pool—there were traces in it of everything. "Oh, no!" she had answered, "of course we should go!"

In the restaurant, still another pool, this time a long narrow one built into the length of the floor, where the dark shapes of the trout twisted slowly back and forth. Everyone made a quip. "Look, they're in their own thermal bath." "Rheumatic trouts, poor things." "Perhaps they need a little radon bath?" She hadn't made her quip yet, so she said, "Now we'll have to choose our victims," and was horrified, but no one seemed to notice.

At the table, Heinrich satirized his own obsession with his cure. In a mock-elderly voice, he gave a little lecture about the healthfulness of eating trout prepared "blue."

"Plain boiled," he said, lifting a finger, "what more can anyone want than that?"

When the waiter came they all humored Heinrich, an agreeable moment, everyone smiling indulgently. Then they sipped wine.

"Heinrich's digestion is unreliable," Elsa said. "His nerves are in a state." Her voice was quick and light. "He works in a publishing house his family owns. Sometimes he writes poetry. It's very good!" Heinrich's melancholy was being visibly broken up, pierced everywhere by bright, deft arrows. "Heinrich and I have been living together in Munich for three years. And"—Elsa never faltered for a minute over this—"Heinrich could not make up his mind to marry. I waited and waited, now there is a child coming."

"So that, of course"—Heinrich's voice, pleasant and open and unembarrassed, broke in—"was the help to deciding."

In the telephone booth of her head a voice said, "It's the right way. You do that too, be more open and that will help." Her husband could sit with this couple and eat a meal and speak of books with them because he thought they were innocent and because they were in the world together, and he was a man who felt responsible to what was in the world, but the rest she must do.

"Sometimes," she said, "my husband and I have trouble looking at Germans or Austrians of a certain age. We think of what they were doing during the Hitler years."

After only the slightest pause, holding their wine midair as if wand-struck, Heinrich and Elsa cried out together, "Yes, yes, that is natural, understandable!" They were dressed in the softest of colors, Heinrich in a pale blue wool sweater and beige slacks, Elsa in a peach knit dress that showed not the least bulge of baby. Her husband was wearing his navy blue jacket with a checked blue shirt open at the throat. The convex metal buttons on his sleeves caught light, and light-formed shapes at the edge of the buttons gave off twisting gleams. She felt his eyes on her.

The dinner arrived. Each fish was covered with a skin that had turned to blue velvet, each was propped, seallike, on the plate, fins like hands supporting the body's upper part, head raised above the curving breast, a mythological creature about to speak: "Consume me and be cured."

For a moment she was afraid she might blurt: "I can't eat this, it's like a character in a children's book!" But she said no such thing. She worked open a snap at the neck of her blouse and waited.

Elsa at once contributed something special to enjoy. "The cheek of the trout is the best part. Not easy to find, though!" Wielding knife and fork precisely, her blond head bent to the task, she folded back a flap of blue velvet in the head of the fish, searched carefully, then put something into her mouth with her fork and looked satisfied. Heinrich also lifted a velvet flap on the head of the fish, poked with his fork and knife, and brought something to his mouth. "Aha."

It was hopeless to try for Elsa's prize; she was not adept with fish, but her husband had the European knack. He began to press a bit of trout against the back of his fork in case of bones. Had he found the small delicacy? She had been staring around the table and might have missed it. She felt certain, somehow, that he hadn't even tried. Why should so silly a thing become an emblem of happiness? Her heart flooded with sorrow for her husband, for what had been stolen from him. If he were Joshua, if she were Joan, she would call out to him, "Find it, oh, please, find it!" Her husband lifted his gaze as if she had spoken, smiling as if to encourage her to find it.

What was it like? The nugget of meat in the little spoon-shaped pelvic bone of the roast chicken? The heart of a boiled artichoke, when you finally got to it, dipped in spicy vinaigrette sauce? The eye of a tiny, butter-soft, baby broiled lambchop, her favorite meal that her mother had cooked for her again and again all the while she was growing up? Her mouth filled with remembered tastes of things that were rare and delicious, gone in a minute.

—1990

2.   Life Notes

On Living in Two Cultures

When the question is asked: "As a Jew in America, how do you feel living in two cultures?" my answer is that I'm relieved to know that it is only two cultures with which I am struggling. I thought it was more. Two cultures, after all, is only the usual difficulty. We can all cite examples apart from Jewish life. I'll give only two that have recently impressed themselves on me. The first is a friend of my daughter's, a Korean girl, whose father desperately tries to intervene between her and Americanization, although she goes to an American school. She must practice Korean, the way my daughter must practice her Hebrew; she must go to Korean religious services and is forbidden to go to American movies. Some day, her father tells her, they may return to Korea. But even if they don't, he wants her to keep her Korean self intact inside the American one. The second example is that of a brilliant Japanese pianist, twenty-three years old, who has been studying here since he was eighteen, practicing thirteen hours a day, building up and mastering a piano repertory. But he has premonitions, he tells me, that one day he will give up the piano. The music, the instrument itself, is completely western, and he is, after all, Japanese. What does all that mean to him, I ask? It means, aside from a myriad distinctions concerning tonality, pitch, form, and mood, that perhaps he ought to perform while sitting on the floor. Very well. Maybe at some time, after years of carrying such an anguish through thirteen hours of daily practice, he will find a way, like Harpo, to take apart the piano—literally or symbolically—and make of it again a non-percussive stringed instrument which he can play while he sits on the floor.

Who, among Americans—aside from Mayflower people, an ever receding breed—does not live in two cultures?

If I were beginning to write a new novel instead of answering a question in a symposium, I would want to fill in "I" as much as

127

possible, supply the reader with evaluative credentials for "I"'s
views. Even in symposia, it's best to know who it is saying what,
and I can at least do what I say I'd like. In terms, that is, of the
relationship between "I" and Judaism. Because although we are
fond of saying "All Israel is one," we know it isn't.

So then: I was born of an immaculate Jewish conception. That
is, my parents, who were Jews by birth, refrained from intercourse
with the Jewish religion and proudly passed me, in an untainted
state, into the world. Not that we were assimilated. No, we stood
in a proud and terrible place outside the "two cultures." Some
years, my father went to reform services on the extra-special
"high" days. But not my mother, who could not stand even this
skimpy slice of official Jewish life. I think now that she was an early
women's liberationist, at least in Jewish matters. Even then I knew
that she bitterly resented the treatment of women in her mother's
orthodox synagogue—on the one hand, the denial of women's
spiritual life, on the other, the physical wearing down of women
under the burdens of homemaking.

No religion, no philosophy, no language, no literature, no cus-
tom. My parents were giving me all this, and thousands of Jewish
parents were giving the same to *their* children. "No blame," as I
CHING says. These parents were mostly first-born-here-
generation Americans, who had heard about or guessed at the
indignities of pre-Holocaust Jewish life in Europe (seldom were the
glories mentioned: parental compassion inhibits much of the
nostalgia and loss under whose weight we might be crushed if the
irredeemable past were truly made vivid for us). These parents in
America were squeezing, as they thought, the slave from their
souls, and were preserving the souls of their children from intru-
sion.

Naturally, I had a splendid Jewish fantasy life. I was conscious
of a crowd of Jewish geniuses, whose great names lit up in the
ungrudging gentile world and whose genes one might be thought,
after all, to have at least partially inherited. How nice to know that
one was chosen to have good brains. How comfortable not to
know what the brains were supposed to be for.

Here is a recent two-culture experience: In June, I went to the
Phi Beta Kappa exercises at Harvard during Commencement
Week. I wanted to hear Elizabeth Bishop, a poet I admire, follow

the tradition of her Harvard teaching post and read her new Phi Beta Kappa poem.

But before I could hear the poem—a ruminative series of pictures of the bus ride down from Nova Scotia to Boston, in the middle of which a moose comes by and looks in the window—I had first to hear a prayer by a Harvard Doctor of Divinity (an ecumenical prayer to be sure, in which God was addressed and Jesus was tactfully suppressed) and next, selections by the male glee. Here there was no suppression. There were abundant Jesus hymns. Now music, it may have been reasoned, transcends differences. Especially *old* music does. Nevertheless, the message I got that morning was that the intellectual community of scholars was of course Christian. As a Jew I felt, and maybe others in the audience did too, publicly stripped of my affiliation. I wonder what the glee would have sung if Charles Reznikoff, say, or Harvey Shapiro, had somehow been appointed Harvard poet that year.

I am tempted to say, in answer to the question of the symposium, that I live in a Christian America and a secular Judaism. But on this matter who needs another joke?

Now back to the moose poem at the Phi Beta Kappa exercises. It can be assumed, apparently, that Jesus hymns will be universally accepted by the intellectual community in Cambridge, but as a Jewish writer I cannot make assumptions about empathy for Jews among gentiles. Nevertheless, I go on making these assumptions in writing because I know that books themselves become part of the moral atmosphere they depict.

One travels backward, deeper into the heart of things, starting with the anglicized reform (most congregants coming into the reform movement today have little or no Hebrew and cannot, in that sense, be said to have *chosen* reform: they simply have no place else to go) until one comes to the thing itself, *la vrai chose,* life among the observant. There, if you are a woman, you are at once living in two cultures within Judaism itself.

The position of Jewish women in relation to Orthodox Judaism is a mirror image of the already sufficiently distorted image of Jews in relation to the world. Can anyone not be struck by the manner in which Jewish women are maligned within Judaism, and the way that resembles how Jews are maligned in the world? The medieval blood libel against Jews (no doubt it's not so medieval as all that, but persists in modern times, as the popularity of the white-slave-trade-run-by-Jewish-shopkeepers-legend in the South of France shows) is no more primitive than the libel against females that calls women unclean (or wickedly seductive) and forbids their presence among holy objects or men. One does not show more horror of the stranger, or more scapegoating for one's own dark fantasies, than the other. We have come to see that in certain times and classes, women have been the slaves of slaves. May we now also admit that Orthodox Jewish women have been the untouchable's untouchable?

Or has all this given way to something else, and is it now, simply, as one swinging Orthodox rabbi told me, that "men are hornier than women" and have to be protected from sexual arousal? In that case it would appear that all this peek-a-booing through the partitions of the mekhitzah ought to place Orthodox religious fervor on a par with what we now know about the underground erotic life of the Victorians. Women must be truly absorbed into Jewish culture, which is to say, into the mainstream of religious observance and all the central activities that sustain it, before they may have the honor of undertaking the anguish of living in merely two cultures.

Another scene: An ecumenical breakfast sponsored by the "Brotherhood," in the basement of a synagogue. Ecumenical because Orthodox and Conservative and Reform were present. By the end of the morning the Orthodox rabbi had publically referred to the Reform one, before his congregation, as "trafe" and the Reform had privately complained that the Orthodox was "a wild man." The Conservative had a chance to shine, middle-of-the-roadness for once taking on transcendent luster:

"I believe in the people of Israel," he chided his colleagues.

I believe in them too, and am longing to see them. Where are they? Now that I have begun my Jewish education I am, naturally, in peril of what a little learning brings. I ask the questions of the foolish daughter. Like, "Where is this 'All Israel' I hear so much about?" All Israel is divided into three packages—neatly wrapped and sealed off. Or if not three then five, or ten. When late but at last I come into some part of Jewish life from my formerly all-American one, garnished by Jewish fantasy, I am reborn not into two cultures but a myriad, all writhing. I am tempted to ask,

"When will 'All Israel' be one so that I can at last share the painful joy of living in only two cultures instead of—say—five?" But on this question, who needs another joke?

Newcomer that I am, I am constantly astonished, overjoyed, to come upon treasures of Jewish thought and literature for the first time. And newcomer that I am, I am constantly brought up short by the split between the nobility of Jewish thought and the vulgarity and chaos of Jewish life.

Nevertheless, I feel as impatient with those who say Judaism is dead as I do, as a writer, with those who say the same about the novel. The novel isn't dead as long as even a handful of practitioners feel moved to use its precincts as a stage on which to figure things out. Judaism had not been a religion with a cast of billions. It has cherished the idea of its fewness (and the world, with brutal humor, is happy to oblige by making the few fewer). Judaism has held aloof—*vide* Rabbi Joseph Soloveitchik's description of Judaism as a "shy" and "retiring" religion.

What is shy and retiring attracts bullies. No need to dwell on this—every form of good attracts a form of evil. Judaism has had an ignorant, destructive press—the worst of it reflecting the only slightly veiled anti-Semitism of Christian teachings.

After the assassinations of Jewish athletes at Munich, the word "tragic" dripped from the pen and lips of every commentator for newspaper, radio and TV, until the world seemed bathed in a great treacle of "tragic." Yet two days after Munich, when the games and scores and ordinary hostilities of the grand sports world had resumed, I heard a Boston TV commentator complain about the judging of the basketball game that reversed a victory for the Americans and gave it to the Russians. The Olympic judges, he said, "stank of righteousness as much as the Pharisees of the Old Testament—I mean the New."

Does this TV commentator understand that the Jewish religion extends beyond the "Old Testament"? Or that the Pharisees slandered in the New Testament are part of it? Or that there is any connection between any of this and the killing in Munich of the eleven Israelis, over whose deaths he had so liberally been pouring the treacle of "tragic"? Is this sportscaster, not too many years away from his schools, the product of religious or of secular Boston? Is there in fact much difference between the two?

This aspect of living in two cultures surely goes beyond the ordinary task of coping with the lapping of the surrounding "gravy" culture against one's personal, favorite culture—of letting in the good and keeping out the bad. Jews—Jews secular, Jews religious, Jews of "All Israel," Jews of not-at-all Israel—live in a world culture that by and large finds the concerns of Jews well outside its powers of empathy.

I find the schizophrenia of the world even deeper than my own. It is not an enjoyable joke.

—1973

Writing as a Woman and a Jew in America

I am a third generation Jewish woman in America, and in the two generations of women who preceded me I have known two violently opposed extremes.

Writing, woman, Jew. I name them in the order of discovery. From an early age I knew that a writer was what I wanted to be. Love of words gave me the patience, and acute shyness the desperate need to figure out a way of communicating other than face-to-face. I add to that a certain ruthlessness.

I am thinking of an act of vandalism when I was eight or nine, and engaged in making a book. I had seen a large letter B in another book, and I fancied it for mine. I therefore cut out half a page from Volume I of *The Book of Knowledge* that stood in splender along with thirteen other volumes in a bookcase of its own (there were no other books or bookcases) in the hall of my grandparents' house.

The heavy weight of the book, the important dark-blue binding and gold-stamped lettering, the smell of thick coated pages, lavishly illustrated—didn't they freeze me with awe? Not for a moment, though I was at other times a careful, anxious child. Was this a symbolic act, then? Was there transcendent significance in excision from a book of knowledge? What about the capital B, itself standing for Book? Was I showing childish ambition to usurp my betters by dismembering the pages on which some of them appeared? Unfortunately, the book I remember making was a scrapbook of movie stars. The B stood for Bette, as in Bette Davis.

So far as I remember, I was never punished for the vandalism, though it was known. I occupied the privileged position of the first and for a long time the only American grandchild in that house of my immigrant grandparents.

Somewhere else in this house there must also have been a Hebrew prayer book. I hadn't known about it and couldn't have used it for my purpose if I had. But I sometimes wonder whether an act of vandalism involving the prayer book would have brought from my grandparents anything other than the tolerant smile I received.

There was no woman's liberation movement, no consciousness-raising going on when I graduated from a woman's college and moved directly into the feminine mystique time of the fifties. Although I was determined that my main efforts would be directed to writing, and all jobs and career efforts would be secondary to that, it sometimes weighed on me that I had not elected to move to the suburbs and create a houseful of children. And when it didn't weigh on me it weighed on my mother.

At that time, in those years, while it certainly wasn't only Jewish families who wanted to marry off their daughters young, I think it would have helped me if I could have known about a Jewish-American writer named Anzia Yezierska, who came as a poor immigrant from Poland in the early 1900s to the Lower East Side, earning pennies with which to stay alive while she realized her burning desire to become an educated woman and a writer. In one of her stories, a young unmarried woman rushes into a room and cries out: "Don't you worry yourself for me. Don't take pity on my years. . . . In America if a girl earns her living she can be fifty years old and without a man, and nobody pities her."

As for being a Jew, it still astonishes me to think of what a long way around I have taken to come there.

The grandparents I knew, the ones who were so lenient with me when I destroyed a book in the only library they owned, were Yiddish-speaking immigrants from Eastern Europe. By the time I knew my grandfather, he had given up religious observance and devoted himself to being an American. As far as I could see, that meant attending to business and listening to Gabriel Heatter and Lowell Thomas, radio commentators, interpret the evening news. My grandmother held on to Jewish observance longer. She lit Shabbos candles, and returned home from shul very late on Yom Kippur, while her children protested that she was overdoing things.

My parents cut through the remaining threads of religious attachment. When I asked my mother about the history of our family—I knew my grandparents intimately: after all I had helped them with their English night school homework, but what about the ones who came before them; surely there was once a time in another country where they were at home and spoke the language?—my mother replied in a way that somehow gave me to understand I was better off not knowing.

Therein lies a key. Say to a child, "Such knowledge is not for you," and the child is instantly off on a quest, as in a fairy tale or legend. The legend I am thinking of is the one where the King and Queen banish spindles from their Kingdom for fear their daughter will prick her finger. But lo and behold there remains one spindle hidden away in a topmost room. Their daughter encounters it, finds it strangely fascinating, tries it, pricks her finger, and the prophecy is fulfilled.

In my case prophecy took a long time to fulfill.

I remember a hunger for some kind of idea-framework against which to place my questions about life. When I was fifteen I asked my father to tell me something about what being Jewish meant. He answered with a sentence. "Do justly, love Mercy, and walk humbly with thy God." Years later, I saw that it was from Micah and that it is sometimes carved over the doorways of Reform synagogues. I think it must have been from one of these that my father read—and memorized—that wisdom. The thought of his committing the line to memory is something that touches me deeply now, but meant nothing to me then.

I asked my father to take me to a synagogue on Rosh Hashanah. He sometimes went on high holy days. My mother wouldn't set foot in one. She expressed scorn for those shuls of her mother's day, places that put women upstairs in hot balconies, far from sight and sound of what was going on, where gossip and noise were the temptation. The rabbi gives a sharp rap on wood with his knuckles, calls for silence! Who's at fault? The women, of course, up there, can't keep their tongues from wagging or their attention focused in the heat and chatter. It was from all this that my mother was shielding me.

My father agreed to go. But somehow he must have gotten the time wrong. It's hard for me now to recapture or express or even fully understand the desolation of my feeling when we arrived. At the very moment when we stood just a few yards from the synagogue, its doors opened and the building began to empty itself of hundreds of people. It seemed to me, standing there with my father, as if all the Jews in the world were walking together in a single community, smiling, embracing, calling out greetings to one another, and that only my father and I were excluded from this belonging. We stood without speaking, while the great Jewish tide passed us by.

Chapel was compulsory at Mount Holyoke, the New England woman's college I attended. During hymn-singing, some religious nerve I didn't know I had was twanged. I perceived I was a Christian, moved to tears by thoughts of Jesus. Since I felt, in the matter of religious observance, immaculately conceived, I naturally could take any form I wanted.

The same nerve twanged again when a European Jew described his family's observances. Jews who loved their Jewishness? What a fascinating piece of news that was! The news was late. By the time I heard about my husband's European parents they had long since died in the Holocaust.

I had come into my knowledge of the Holocaust and Jewish identity at the same moment. And the knowledge of the former sank into swift and bitter full circle with the latter just in time to darken it, nearly to blot it out, as in an eclipse. My efforts to study and to learn since then, to inform my writing with deeper knowledge of Jews, not only in the accidents of their sociology but in their enduring attachments to the search for belief and meaning—what else are they but an effort to insert my mind into the little space left between the shining of the sun and its darkening?

One story of a Jew's return that moves us is the one about Franz Rosenzweig, the Jewish philosopher, born of an assimilated German-Jewish family. As a young man he decided, like many of his friends, to convert to Christianity. Being historically minded, he saw that for him it was necessary to first become a Jew, and proceed from there as the early Christians had done. On Yom Kippur eve, therefore, the story goes, he sought out a synagogue that housed a small Orthodox Polish-Jewish congregation. He stood among them, prayed as they did, felt the fervor they felt, and saw that he need go no further. He became an Orthodox Jew. He became Franz Rosenzweig, the Jewish philosopher.

But I think, too, about Simone Weil, also a philosopher, also born into an assimilated Jewish family, this one in Paris. She, too, wanted to convert to Christianity. But so anti-Jewish were her feelings that they actually stood in the way. No priest would convert her because she would have become an instant Christian heretic, one who denied the Judaic component of the Judeo-Christian tradition. She preferred her Christianity to be pure Greek.

Nevertheless, sometimes I like to fantasize that somehow Simone Weil might also have visited a synagogue full of Jewish fervor. Alas, what could have happened there? She would not be gathered in among the devout near the Torah, but shunted aside, made to sit apart, and from this distance would have observed with the eyes only, instead of with heart and mind. She would have emerged as alienated as she entered.

Perhaps, though in another way, I share my mother's anger with synagogue establishments. I am angry for the loss of the Jewish philosopher, Simone Weil.

Recently, I came across an old literary magazine in which there was a symposium called "The Writer's Sense of Place." Many of the contributors were Southern writers and one, Carson Mc-Cullers, wrote this: "The voices reheard from childhood have a truer pitch. And the foliage—the trees of childhood—are remembered more exactly."

That seemed apt but expected. Another writer, the poet Richard Eberhardt, said more interestingly that for him place existed not in geography but in vision: "A place is a fusion of human and natural order, and a peculiar window on the whole. . . . The imagination . . . seeks the invisible through the visible."

When I began to write, I saw to my surprise that for me place, vision, imagination—all the elements that formed my peculiar window—concerned Jews.

Even a novel set in an abortion clinic, *At the Center,* which developed out of a series of interviews for the *New York Times Magazine,* did not come together for me as novel until I could begin to see it from a Jewish aspect. After I had published my article I felt haunted by the material. In the interviews, conflicting voices had spoken from among physicians, clinic administrators, patients, families—all those figures who hover about the woman.

The idea for the book then began to take shape as a chorus of voices. Reading through rabbinic responses on abortion, I was moved to see how many rabbis struggled to find in favor of the woman. Whatever endangered her well-being, even mental anguish, could be considered grounds for abortion. In *At the Center* a pious couple who have already lost a family in the Holocaust come to America and join a Hassidic community. Their daughter, Hannah, born into this community, strains against its limitations but stays on out of pity for her parents and their hopes for her. One day the two old people are robbed and strangled in their apartment. In her bitterness Hannah finds the means to flout God. Deliberately she breaks Halachic law after law—dietary laws, laws of sexual purity, whatever is in her power to do. This is what she thinks:

> Once or twice a great rabbi of the past had argued with God. One, after a bloody destruction, had even thrown stones up at heaven. But women? They were not on record as doing anything much but beseeching and weeping. When Biblical Hannah prayed in the Temple for fertility, swaying in her fervor, the priest had pronounced her drunk. Let Him hear for a change a woman's voice.
>
> Arguments with men God sometimes seemed to enjoy—with Abraham, with Moses, with Lot, with Jonah. Up to a point. But with women? About this there was no news. She would see . . . what the end of her argument would be. . . . Her pen, like Balaam's tongue, somehow pours out only praise and hope. Therefore her voice would be in the kitchen, slicing cheese with a meat knife; under the Sabbath candles, writing . . . ; in the lover's bed.
>
> She reflects that some might think her belief that she could engage the Deity in dispute no more than self-delusion. "But is what I think so different," she asks herself, "from what men do? They take off their prayer shawls and tell themselves they've had their say.

Hannah is not only a sort of recording angel (if fallen), but a shaper of events. She sees God, the world, Jews, herself, in a new light by the end of the book. And making use of an image that comes from Jewish mysticism, she sees herself, her body, as a kind of sacred Succah, in which the heart is the etrog and the spine the lulov. Her own being will be a stopping place for her in her dangerous and desirable Jewish journey.

—1983

Friday Night Fever

Here we are a writer's group composed of Jewish women and someone suggests we have an all-women's shabbos meal together on Friday night and I ask does anybody feel uncomfortable about leaving the family, after all it's a family night? There's a bad silence and then one woman says if we think that way we might as well be back in the Ark. I wonder for a second what that means—the Ark. Back in covenanted times? What's so bad about that? No, back two by two, she must mean. That's bad? Well, all right it's bad if there's no choice. I can see that—some might want to go alone, or in threes, say. But I notice this woman's married. I notice because toward the end of the evening when I go for my coat I see this quiet, balding man sitting out in the front hall, drinking water from a paper cup he must have gotten from the bathroom. He's absolutely non-threatening, smiles at me humbly, and says nothing. I introduce myself, and he answers that he's Lillian's husband. Well, the meeting's just about over, I say, why doesn't he join them inside for coffee? No. He smiles, perfectly accepting. He knows they want to be just all women together. He's what's known in the husband trade as a sweetie. I can't help wondering if he's Jewish, this man Lillian chose to go with her two by two. Some of the women say they know they're Jewish because they know at least one of their parents was and that's as much as they know. Some, not even that much. One woman says she didn't know till she was twenty-one, her parents kept it from her. We're supposed to be writing, under this grant, about what it means to us to be Jewish and mostly what gets written are stand-up-comic skits, the kind Jewish men write, only these are about women, about their being attracted to handsome blond lovers who do or don't respond to their dark ethnic looks. Every once in a while someone will ask, but is that Jewish? Of course, comes the answer, it's Jewish because you're Jewish. I'm not trying to sound superior. I'm in the same

boat (it's not the Ark), the only difference is that I somehow married a man who knows some Jewish history and ritual and wants to keep it in his life, our life. It isn't that he'll have a fit if I go to a women's shabbos on Friday night, it's that he'll really notice that it's Friday and I'm not there. So then, do I really want to do that? Do I want to take away meaning from one place in order to transfer it to another place? Isn't the idea to *add* to the locations of meaning? If I go to the women's shabbos, then I can't be at the family shabbos. Of course, I see that's back in the Ark, two by two, that's not right either. Noah and his wife (did she also have no name like Lillian's husband?) and their children got jammed into the Ark for a while because they had to be. Eventually the doors were opened and they were all let loose. That's when they got free will back again, which is what's making it so hard right now to decide where to have shabbos or what really makes a Jewish play.
                                                                     —1987

A Women's Service

One Sabbath morning a Learned Woman, along with a little band of equally Learned Women, called for me at my home in a Boston suburb.

From Brookline, we began our walk in the direction of Cambridge. Into the town of Alston, past the clutter of buildings and stores and nothing to refresh the spirit except a wedge of pizza from "The Leaning Tower of . . . ," which of course we don't avail ourselves of, the latest flavor of ice cream from the local Brigham's, which we likewise eschew.

Up the steep ramp of the Cambridge Street Bridge we lean, past the New England architectural motif of workers' quarters—three-family frame houses with three-tier corner porches facing, wherever it can be managed, it seems, the repair lot of a gas and auto-service station. On we walk. At last we see ivy-clutched Harvard buildings. Curves of football stadium, mews, closes, yards above which domes of green, blue, and gold raise their heads so high in the Harvard air that the winds that play above them speak only to weather-vaned roosters and cods. Oh, the painful triumph and triumphant pain of this Sabbath not-riding! Grimed Harvard athletes grunt and sweat through the rules of their game with no idea that this little limping group beyond the cyclone fence (the Learned Woman and her hobble-footed friends) are moving by rules of a different kind. Past burning feet we walk. Past the rub of nylon stockings on the plastic innersoles of pumps. Past blisters. Past the squeeze of the bunion joint, that foot-bound Chinese princess of no-running, until we appear to be stepping high, like Tennessee Walking Horses, out of our own feet for very tenderness. We might have carried sneakers but carrying is forbidden.

We come at last to Hillel House in Somerville, into a room full of women, and piled-up sheets of xeroxed paper. In Hebrew.

"I'm afraid I can't . . . ," I say.

"I'll translate for you," says the Learned Woman. "These are quotes from two rabbis of ancient times. The first said, 'It is commanded to you to teach Torah to your daughter.' The second, 'He who teaches Torah to his daughter, it is as though he had taught an idiot.'"

"Why both?" I ask.

The Learned Woman tilts her head and smiles. "This is what we start from."

Below the sayings, some lines of prayer. The Learned Woman explains what lies between those lines. "The traditional blessings are said by men. They have the responsibility of saying them daily. For women, for us, other words have been substituted."

I ask what would happen if women said the same words as the men, and whether that would seem ridiculous to people, as if women dressed themselves like firemen and ran to a house that wasn't burning, rushed out in trucks, ran up ladders, hosed with water a house in which there was no fire.

"Jewish life has been in flames for centuries, that's true," the Learned Woman answers judiciously.

But Jewish women, I gather, have been told these are not their flames. "And certainly," I say, "this is not their hose? No hose, no blessing?"

"Hold off," the Learned Woman answers, smiling, "on your questions, if you can, till after the service." She consults her watch and says she hopes they start on time. Then she motions that they are about to begin.

The Ark that holds the Torah is a brown cupboard on a card table. There is another table, with its hind legs folded under itself and resting on a tall narrow box. The wide black stripes and knotted fringes of the prayer shawl that covers the table come near to touching the floor.

"That's the reader's lectern," the Learned Woman whispers. "They've tried to provide a proper reading angle for the Torah when it's set on the table."

Now a tall, slender woman removes the Torah from the Ark. As she turns with her burden to face the company of women, she begins to sing in a clear, high voice. Her face and body are almost painfully thin. She has been chosen for this moment, no doubt, because of the purity of her voice, but is it also, somehow, for the fragility and narrowness of her wrists and fingers? How heavily the heavy Torah body rests on that skinny hand whose knob of wristbone juts out like a cracked stone!

Now this mad Quixote of a woman—who insists on carrying a burden that everyone has told her is not her burden—walks, singing, among the women. They touch the scroll cover with their fingertips, then their fingertips to their lips. Or some touch the binding of the book they hold to the Torah covering and then kiss the book.

All goes slowly. The Torah is undressed, laid upon the table, and opened. Each young woman who is called up adds the name of her mother to the customary naming of the father. The Learned Woman, shifting her energetic little body from foot to foot as she stands next to me, sighs and whispers, "At this rate, they'll never get through."

In fact we can hear, from the men's service in the next room, that the chanting and singing are going on at a far brisker pace. The scroll is scanned within now, with the aid of a silver finger, by one after another of these young women. They chant, sing, bow low over the words. Another slim person, a short one this time, in a short pleated skirt, lifts the Torah, holds it high and walks with it. Then she sits down, hard, under the Torah's weight, on one of the straight wooden chairs. She balances the two points of the scroll-sticks on her thighs. Still another woman begins to dress the scroll. Gently lowering the blue velvet garment with its gold fringe hem over the double curve of the Torah-body, smooth-skinned, standing curled into itself upon its stick-legs. The silver breastplate and neck-chain are hung upon the shoulders of the scroll. The silver crowns mounted, with bells. Then the Torah, like a precious child, heavy and not able to walk, is carefully, lovingly, handed to another young woman. The walking and the singing begin again.

Though rhythms and pitches and melodies convey their message, shut out from understanding, I long for an illuminating ray of English.

However, none of this matters. From the moment the tall, skinny young woman turned to face us with the Torah heavy on her arm, I have felt tears streaming down my cheeks. Oh, the way that has been lost! The voice, the poems, the burdens women seek that have not been their burdens! I am mystified by my grief. I had not been longing for burdens. . . .

The Learned Woman sighs and shifts on burning feet. She glances at her watch, then joins the prayers and the singing, expertly. (Learned Woman! I am in awe of her.) She sighs again, looks on with interest. Yet it seems to me that the Learned Woman listens with a certain longing to the sudden bursts of song that come from time to time into our slow-chanting room. Bursts that indicate to the Learned Woman (who nudges another woman and taps her watch) the swiftness with which the experienced men next door have dispatched—carried, kissed, undressed, explored, and dressed again—the body of their wisdom-scroll.

"Listen to that," the Learned Woman whispers. She can hear that the men at their own service next door are already near the end, and she comments that the women will have to learn to make things go a little quicker.

"Will they do this now, always?" I whisper past the lump that is plugging my throat.

"Should they?" the Learned Woman whispers back.

I answer that there's no way I can know that, and ask the Learned Woman whether she thinks they should.

"It's a problem," the Learned Woman answers. "They can keep this up and get better at it. . . ."

"Better . . . ?"

"But the weight of tradition is not with them. It's in the next room, with the men. I am for innovation, but I am also for reality."

"Then what will happen to these women—these masters and doctoral candidates? Who will have them? Where will they go, so beautiful in their learning and their singing? What can happen now?"

"Ah, then it did speak to you!" the Learned woman answers, smiling. She says that an ancient rabbi once said that even if you know you can't finish a task you are still obliged to work on it as much as you are able. "Not today, it's shabbos, but another day I'll write out the Hebrew for you so you can learn it."

The Learned Woman and her friends walk their pious way back without me.

—1973

Women? Writers?

An invention: Let us suppose a woman who wants to enter the new territory of feminist thinking through books. She is thirtyish, a homemaker and mother of small children. Let's call her Fredericka, because it is a derivative of a man's name; and let's say that before now she received her image of herself from men. In college, male teachers teaching ideas held by men about "man"; in novels, male authors writing about men as heroes and women as consorts—that sort of thing.

Suppose Fredericka went to the library and asked a friendly librarian to help her sample books on "feminist themes," or maybe the library has thoughtfully arranged shelves of such books. What might Fredericka find?

Impossible to mention them all—all the novelists and poets and heroines and genres and modes and views; all the new young writers and rediscovered older writers and revivals of long-dead ones—that crowd those shelves. So much, it appears, has been pent up for so long. "Who are we?" women—the newly self-conscious group—ask themselves. Fredericka looks through the images provided by writers to find some clues.

Let's suppose that Fredericka is lucky enough to find on the shelves this first visit some of the novels (they go out fast) of sexual revolution and breakthrough. Here are the new heroines who hurl themselves into life and sex with so much intelligence, so much experience, so much experiment that it's as if they had in mind Virginia Woolf's lament and warning: Shakespeare's sister never went anywhere or was allowed to do anything, and so even with Shakespeare's talent, could not have been Shakespeare.

After only a few years of consciousness-raising—which may turn out to be the quickest, cheapest and friendliest form of self-help attitude-reforming in the annals of psychological therapy—not to mention deep-self-scrutiny (physical as well as mental), reading in their own history and other labors, women writers have leaped over the barbed-wire fences to a new sexual honesty and self-exposure.

Not so long ago, any writer worth her salt struggled to write herself free of the epithet, "woman writer." "Damned scribbling women," Hawthorne fumed. Woman writers, sob sisters, the three-named ladies. (I had heard nothing but sneers for the three-named ladies, so I junked my family name—it's gone forever.) Out of the loins of the woman's movement, the term woman writer is born again. Separatist? Regressive? Separatism to end separatism, war to end war. Paradox enough. There is only one literature, that is human literature, and all who can, participate and contribute. Need we repeat—nothing human is alien to me? Yes.

Yet there's no doubt that in the last few years there has been an outpouring of writing by women about women. It is as if the woman's movement gave a kind of support that led to an exuberant letting go, out of imagination or memory. Some of it very good writing, some of it art, some of it confessional and documentary—interesting because the confessed and documented matters haven't been written about before.

So be it. Making a separate category of women writers is a kind of holding pattern then, till themes and responses and methods worked by women are also given safe conduct in the world.

Clearly the atmosphere around women who write is slowly but surely improving. They are freer to create out of a larger range of styles and attitudes than before. And reviews, apart from an occasional dreadful "affirmative action" review, in which a woman is set to review a woman with the obvious purpose of redressing a general wrong instead of addressing a particular book, have gotten a bit more fair-minded toward women.

Still, every writer will have her own list of reviewing grievances from before the enlightenment. Here are mine:

Book I: Reviewer praises it for charm, for playfulness, for being "an idyll . . . about unsuccessful people working for an unsuccessful company . . . [in] go-getting America. . ." But it wasn't "corrosive" enough. (1) Who said I wanted to be corrosive at all? (2) The desire for corrosiveness is an aspect of the received idea that books must be "active," that is, "masculine," that is: "Don't just stand there depicting something and making us see how it works—give it a kick!"

Book II: Review opens with an Anthony Burgess quote: He prefers books with "a strong male thrust, an almost pedantic allusiveness and a brutal intellectual content." Reviewer tries to grope his way out of his own trap: "But surely the appetite for honest emotional goods is not exclusively feminine?"

Book III (this time, alas! a woman reviewer): ". . . One cannot read this novel without stumbling over queries about the female condition. (If only this topic might stay in the garage for a while! It just isn't one of our primary national problems.)"

And now back to the shelves.

Had Fredericka been under the impression that masturbation was exclusively a male, not female, subject in fiction? There is *Marcella,* by Marilyn Coffey, a novel whose content is almost exclusively female adolescent sexuality and masturbation.

Were women supposed to be passive and submissive? There is a new woman who is swashbuckling and adventuring, picaresque, who hunts adventure and men. Fredericka takes out Erica Jong's *Fear of Flying* and finds that the heroine adores males with all the fervor Humbert lavished on Lolita, and rivals his passion with hers for male bodies, male smells, male ejaculations.

Were women supposed to be masochists? The new heroine seeks pleasure and is the first to walk out when it wanes, as Alix Kates Shulman's heroine does in *Memoirs of an Ex-Prom Queen.*

Were they supposed to be "ladylike," modest in speech and manner? Then what used to be called "locker-room talk" would be welcomed into the house, and women would speak it as easily as men.

Fredericka staggers home with her load of books and finds herself admiring. How brave these women are! They defy the father, the husband; they defy the analyst himself! They are all, these heroines, wound into analysis and analysts (Lois Gould's novel is called *Final Analysis*)—married to them, having affairs with them, telling their stories to them, *seeing through them* ("You see, you must now learn to agzept yourzelf as a vooman . . . ").

Without masochism, who would be analyzed? Who would pay to be flogged? Those heroines, having cut themselves off from one unsatisfactory safety, the husband, want to hold themselves back from running to the next; to refuse also the trap of unsatisfactory liaison with analyst. Unless it is analyst as lover, in which case analyst is stripped down to full pomposity. In *Fear of Flying*, the analyst-lover leads the heroine in a week-long romp through the woods without timetable in order to teach her how to give herself to existential life, then leaves abruptly for his next appointment.

They hack away, these women, at the ground under their own feet, sacrificing the old ways of safety, forcing themselves to face the void. Mapless and chartless, at the close of their books they are deep into their own hair—they have cut it and it will never be the same, or they are brushing it, waiting for the next encounter to see if they will still be brave. (It is not easy to end a book for which the cry is—Make it new!) And in Doris Lessing's *The Summer Before the Dark*, a woman in midlife lets *her* hair, formerly dyed and coifed, go gray and unruly. She is through with cosmetics and seductiveness, that expression of dependence.

Feeling exhilarated and also liberated, without yet having done anything, Fredericka goes back to the library for more. Oddly enough, it is within one of the most militantly ideological groups of writers—black writers—that she finds there are women who are looking back, recreating the experience of mothers and grand-mothers. The heroines do not feel the panic of dependence on men—in that sense, they are the exception to and reversal of the portraits of white women—and are shown often as radiant centers for confused offspring and sullen lovers.

One of these writers, Alice Walker, searches for images of her own that will restore grandeur to the old black women who were the "mules" of the world, and finds creativity in their humble doings—their quilts, their gardens, their songs, their Bible reading. (Women novelists who are Jewish have so far refrained from this act of reparation toward their mothers, and are still finding them good for a laugh, much as male writers have done. So far, Mrs. Portnoy is getting no more sympathetic understanding from her daughters than from her sons about the pressures that shaped *her* life.)

Fredericka browses through an anthology, *By a Woman Writt*, and reads the laments of women against their dependent condition from as far back as six centuries ago.

She finds the work of May Sarton, indefatigable writer of novels, memoirs, poems, whose recurring theme is woman and solitude—a new idea for Fredericka: she had been used to thinking about women as both blessed and cursed by community, roiling life. Solitude had seemed the most masculine of domains. Women never went up to the mountain or into the desert to get in touch with themselves and/or eternity. In Sarton's books, they did.

She finds volumes of Anaïs Nin's ongoing journal, a forty-year-long monologue of analysis and description: dreams, conversations, fantasies—what Nin calls "woman's own cycles, storms, terrors. . . ."

She finds works by two fiction writers who have published so little that their appearance in one year is something of a startling coincidence: Tillie Olsen and Grace Paley. Both these writers have given, publicly, extenuating reasons for their long silences, which may have as much to say about the condition of women as their published work. These have to do with the events of their time and the demands made on domesticated women's lives. (Remember how, in *Armies of the Night*, Norman Mailer begs off from some protest activism because he has a magazine deadline to meet?)

Tillie Olsen bestows an extraordinary tenderness on her own characters—in her newly published *Yonnondio,* as well as in her earlier *Tell Me a Riddle*. Whether they are at the bottom of the working class, or intellectuals, she gives them her own gifts—the same capacities that she herself possesses for reverent attention to beauty, to wonder, to personality, to the details of the moment.

Grace Paley's tone is wry, where Olsen's is almost elegaic. The women in her stories are full of a kind of absentminded knowledge, as women are who need to turn off from too many demands. Longing to be gone, yet they hang around, remarkably without rancor.

An eerily haunting book by Iris Owens, *After Claude,* takes up again the theme of dependency, this time bringing it to its absurd and terrifying conclusion. At first, the tone is comedy. A sharp-eyed and witty young woman easily pierces through the pomposities of the men who strut around her. In fact, throughout the book, she never meets a man she doesn't despise. Still she cannot give up her lunatic hanging on. Her premise is that she must not be on her own, and her attitude keeps switching back and forth between panicked pursuing and scornful deflating. Without guile or the knack of lies, she is like some semi-evolved creature stuck somewhere on its way out of the ooze, flapping legless on land with gills instead of lungs.

In the end, dependency wins over clear-sightedness. She falls into the hands of one of those evil "families" headed by insane father-figures, and is on her way to total enslavement.

Fredericka then comes upon the novels of Joyce Carol Oates, about whom she's heard it said that she writes "the social novel." But she finds Oates is in fact writing out of the inside of her own head like every other real writer. Fredericka finds her disconcertingly good at delineating states of unconsciousness in women who act violently and never know why, or are passive and never know why. *Do With Me What You Will*, the title of one of her books, might be the title of all of them. Her characters are sleepwalkers, and their somnambulistic paths (usually to hell) are meticulously traced.

If Oates's characters seldom know why they suffer, the poets, so good at naming things, tick if all off.

Fredericka reads Sylvia Plath, the lists of numbing dreads: "Viciousness in the kitchen! / The potatoes hiss," and: "I am no drudge / Though for years I have eaten dust / And dried plates with my dense hair. / And seen my strangeness evaporate, / Blue dew from dangerous skin;" And: "I know why you will not give it to me, / You are terrified / The world will go up in a shriek, and your head with it. . . ."

Adrienne Rich links the insensibility of a country with its own insulted and injured: "For weeks now a rage / has possessed my body, driving / now out upon men and women / now inward upon myself / . . . in a world masculinity made / unfit for women or men . . . " and: "I suddenly see the world / as no longer viable: / you are out there burning the crops / with some new sublimate. . . ."

Reading Rich, Fredericka thinks of the bullet-headed Lairds and Rusks of Washington. Thinks of George Grosz cartoons, of official cruelty everywhere, that passes for the rigors of *realpolitik*. The woman-voice in the poems perceiving this is a creature driven near to madness by horror, by the frustrating of every life-nurturing impulse. The world is on a death trip, this sensibility records. She will soon join it in the ultimate despair—in madness and suicide.

And so round again to Sylvia Plath, to the horror broken out past language—the real suicide, the head in the oven, the babies wailing in their cots. . . .

Very shaken, very puzzled, very discouraged, Fredericka stops reading for a while and thinks again about the group of irrepressible novels about adventuring women with which she began her reading.

Two extremes—where does she place her own life? She sees, suddenly, how full those earlier, flamboyant novels are of money. A passage from Jong's novel sounds now depressingly like the class notes of some wealthy alumnae quarterly:

"In June, we left for Europe together. Charlie was going to a conducting competition in Holland; I had friends to visit in Yorkshire, was due to meet my old buddy Pia in Florence for a jaunt through southern Europe, and was going to see my sister Randy in the Middle East. Charlie and I planned to stay in Holland together for two weeks and then part company. He was supposedly going home to conduct an oratorio at some arts festival. . . ."

Fredericka is not a psychiatrist. She and her husband (who is also not a psychiatrist) struggle with a brutal inflation that hardly allows baby-sitting money after food and rent are paid for. And there we leave Fredericka for now, still putting casseroles in the oven (for the time being) instead of her head.

A few years back, I wrote myself a baffled note about certain women writers. They were strongly intellectual, satiric, witty. Yet not once in the worlds of these writers' books was a character created that might equal the spiritual stature we suspected was in the creator herself. The characters mostly represented meanness of spirit, and the events in these novels consisted of all the exciting deviltry that mean spirits were capable of.

The women created by Mary McCarthy, for example, are clever but nowhere intelligent enough. Nothing like, say, the intellectual dimension of McCarthy herself. Why was that? Why was it none of these women had created a character whose inner life approached anything like the scope or the range of possibility of the creator's own? Survival with integrity, with intactness and with discipline were nowhere represented in their fiction. Was that because moral virtue does not make enough of an impact? Is less of an "assault" upon reality?

Was it possible that even the great McCarthy had at some time said to herself, "I will not write like a woman"? Were women novelists always saying secretly to themselves, "I will not write like a woman writer"?

And what is this taken-for-granted, writing-like-a-woman? Do we know what it is? We know what it isn't. For years, the sexist compliment: she writes like a man. That meant tough; muscular prose, no emotional abreacting, explicit about sex.

Few men followed that recipe. Norman Mailer, Hemingway's most visible, self-announced disciple, had been evolving a style that every year put out additional tendrils, vines and creepers, so that he had come more and more to resemble Dorothy Richardson, that first interior monologuist whose prose was given over to "womanly flow." Nevertheless, the standard came down heavy on women. Do we know how women would write if this were not so?

Virginia Woolf's essay called *Mr. Bennett and Mrs. Brown* purported to address itself to the Edwardian novelist, Arnold Bennett, to chastise him for thinking the truth about human beings resided in outward, material reality—what one bought, where one went, how much was spent, and what happened then. Truth, Woolf said, rested in the moment, in inner awareness and subjective response to it. Not what was there in "reality," but how somebody felt about it.

She was clearing the way for a new sensibility. Her manifesto was a combination, as such things always are, of her own bent— the way she herself saw things—with the literary moment. She announced that naturalism was a played-out form.

Woolf herself was later dismissed as old guard by her compatriot, Graham Greene. He addressed her in an essay in which he declared, "Regent Street is real." The novel of subjectivity was played out, he said. Objective reality, so long neglected by the Bloomsbury group, cried for expression. He was cleverly unifying his own preference for books of plot and action (reflecting, as he said, his favorite childhood reading) with the cultural *Zeitgeist*.

Literature is often a matter of response to the challenge of the literature that went before. Work by women swings not only on this pendulum, as most writing does; it swings on a second pendulum, within the first. Women reply to what is expected of them as women—complying if they are compliant, rebelling if not. At the moment, the novelists of sexual freedom and adventure are replying with role reversals in order to prove that women can exist in the world of sex-cum-politics-cum power.

Sex sells. What, in the end, will prevent the exploitation of sex in women's books, exactly as has happened with men's? How will women writers avoid the general corruption—now that they are coming out explicitly about sex—of a book trade that pushes sex and violence, of publishers who pander while piously lamenting . . . ?

The time between revolution and counterrevolution is shorter every year (think of the flower-children rags now hanging expensively on Fifth Avenue racks). How long will it be before courageous breakthrough hardens into the expected? Or the obligatory?

Still, there's no point worrying in advance, when there's so much else that's already here. Namely, something that's been working in the tone of American writing for some time. It might all have to do with Ezra Pound or Hemingway and their ruthless suppression of certain feeling words (and with them, certain feeling states). Oddly enough, poets seem to have slid out from under that thumb and to have moved far from the dry Eliotic tone. But fiction has not gotten off so easily. In the opening page of *Augie March,* Saul Bellow replies to Hemingway: ". . . if you hold down one thing you hold down the adjoining." And he proceeded to write the most expansive, inclusive book in American letters since Mark Twain, using comedy to get at material otherwise too painful to approach. American novelists appeared to follow suit, but in fact most of them have replied to the call for feeling-in-writing with the kind of comedy that points to nothing but itself. Seemingly confessional and open, the tone of American novels has been getting slicker, glibber, funnier. Stand-up comics, our novelists have become. The comedy used not as a means of getting at feeling, as it properly should, but as feeling-barrier. Nothing is merely funny any more, it is "wildly" funny, as if comedy were an end in itself. And this is largely the state of fiction by males at the moment when some women writers wish to emulate, usurp, or redo it in female clothing.

Paradoxically, a few male novelists are now writing novels of sensibility and subjectivity (William Gass is one). Some write under the fresh impetus of the "new novel" in France, of which Nathalie Sarraute, evoker of Virginia Woolf, is a practitioner. But few women in America want, or dare, to write that way.

Still and all, I argue with myself, what if there is a certain amount of backlash writing by women, what's wrong with it? Isn't it important to do that, not only to show the accusers—the men—that it can be done, but also to show women readers? To give, as the saying now goes, "role models" to countless women suffering in their dependent situations, lacking courage to live other lives? To Fredericka, say?

For answer, I turn to a panel discussion at the recent National Book Award festivities. At one moment, the Gothic novel came in for shaming. Romantically false, betrayer of liberation, not to mention literature, it has been written by women for women for years, and still is. A brave woman stood up and admitted that she was such an author. She defended the right of these books to exist. "My Aunt Ella reads them," she said. "She'll never read anything else and there are thousands of women like her. They need them!"

So there it was again. In a totally unexpected way, the swaggering "female machismo" novel suffers from the same trouble as the saccharine embarrassing romance. Both tell less than the whole truth because people have to be helped, or because they need a supplement, a vitamin that's missing from their reading diets, and women writers help them out, responding to need, fighting back at attackers, to prove, to show.

Do men writers do this? Do they worry about providing "role models" in their books? Does Nabokov care whether Humbert Humbert sets the image of men-as-lovers back a thousand years? Or even back forty—to the time when as little boys they played doctor with little girls?

And yet another, less flamboyant aspect of role-model books. For some the women's movement has meant a call to tract writing, sweetened with fictional effects. These are the hardest to talk about without seeming to turn against what is so bravely meant. But the truth is, fiction dies under the duress of ideology.

Some years ago, Doris Lessing's *The Golden Notebook* was published. It was a rich and original piece of work, full of insights into the condition of women and men, with and without each other. But *The Summer Before the Dark,* published by Lessing after the women's movement had arrived, was thoroughly didactic and programmatic. The heroine's inner life and reflective powers existed only to the extent they were needed to solve the problems at hand, and the insights were as skin-deep as the abandoned cosmetics.

Numbers of recent novels end with the protagonist drawing a deep breath and saying, in effect, "I see what I must do. My life will never be the same after this" (having a baby, a divorce, an analysis, an affair . . .). Like Stephen Hero, they are off to forge in the smithy of their souls the uncreated conscience of their race. What could be nobler? Straight talk and straight dealing with these matters are in order. It would be monstrous if writers were to bypass these human questions for the sake of esthetics. Unthinkable to have no part in the long journey of humanity toward itself, that strenuous up-current leaping.

The question of the depth at which and from which one writes concerns art, important not for snobbish or elitist reasons, but because it alone provides the means for plumbing the place where difficulties lie. Difficulties in turn force out the methods of the deep. And so it goes, this struggle between the deep and the diver, each squeezing more and more out of the other, and at ever deeper levels. Sometimes it's the deep that wins. And then there is no triumphant going off to forge anything in the smithy of one's soul.

Freedom! Freedom! What else can it mean except the freedom to risk all that to write without worrying what "they" will think? Everything we do or don't do is political whether we like it or not—hard-won wisdom of the age. But in that case a subtly shaded, idiosyncratic life, lived moment to moment (or died) in the light, clear or dim, of its own sweet (or stinking), mysterious (always), integrated (or falling-apart) self is also political. Maybe even more political. Maybe that is the most astoundingly political life a person can live. Maybe if we were free to write about that. . . .

How many swings of the pendulum within the pendulum will it take before women can write as freely as this? How many brave but ultimately irrelevant books must they first write to prove women can do what men have done?

A whole area of idiosyncratic response has been scorned and

suppressed in writing, or reduced to the despised status of "female sensibility." When this is no longer true, or at least when we free ourselves to write as if it were no longer true, then we will be on our way toward creating a literature of which it can at last be said: Women have put their hand to it, and something new has come into books.

As for Fredericka, she is beginning now to read the theorists. First, Betty Friedan who holds the mirror up to the emperor's clothes—the feminine mystique, said by the world to possess great spiritual qualities, but in fact utterly without respect or value in the eyes of the world. Next, on to Kate Millett's exposure in *Sexual Politics,* quote by quote, of the great (male) novelists and their slander of women. Finally, to Germaine Greer's *The Female Eunuch.* "If women understand by emancipation the adoption of the masculine role then we are lost indeed." And: "Most of the defects pointed out by critics of women are simply the results of their having been sheltered from the subtler and more effective types of enculturation which their society lavished upon its male leaders." And: "To heal is to make whole, as in wholesome; to make one again; to unify or reunify; this is Eros in action."

So the Messiah was to be a woman, after all. As usual, the Messiah tarries. Meanwhile, from so much reading, Fredericka's attitudes have been slowly changing. She expects more from herself in the way of some kind of achievement or work outside her home. One of these days, she may just decide to write a book. . . .

—1974

On the Dearth of Female Intellectuals

"The search for writers who are intellectuals and women is a tough one," Norman Mailer said at the PEN Congress. Writer-intellectuals were what was wanted for the panels, but few women could be found to fill the bill. As if to underscore female indifference to matters of mind, a number of women who merited invitations did not even bother to show up.

My dictionary defines an intellectual as "one who professes or is supposed to possess enlightened judgment and opinions with respect to public or political questions." Already somewhat elderly, my dictionary says that to use the term simply as applying to the mental faculties is downright archaic.

But what about applying it to poets and novelists?

Poets, essayists, novelists—those are the writers of whom PEN in its literary core is composed. Can they—men or women—yield what's needed? Do they—women or men—want to? Who or what is an intellectual writer or writer-intellectual?

"No ideas but in things," said the poet William Carlos Williams. The novelist transposes that to: No ideas but in character and act. "Squeeze the slave from the soul," said Chekhov, meaning slavery of intellect, of course, as well as of spirit.

Some writers do engage in what the dictionary says intellectuals do. But when they are doing it, are they writing as poets and novelists? Clearly not. Julio Cortazar told how it was with him when he was seized by a story: ". . . for no *reason*, without warning, without the warning aura of epileptics, without the contractions that precede severe migraines, without anything that gives him a chance to clench his teeth and take a deep breath, *he is a story*, a shapeless mass without words or faces or beginning or end, but still a story, something that can only be a story, and then, suddenly, Tanzania can go to hell, because he puts a paper in the

typewriter and begins to write, even if his bosses and the whole
United Nations scream in his ears. . . ."

Are these the words of a writer-intellectual, or an intellectual at
all, or simply a writer of stories?

When E. L. Doctorow was irritated by the presence of Secretary of State Shultz at PEN he wrote an op-ed piece in protest. But
elsewhere, about the real writing, novel writing, writing on the
basis of which he was invited to join PEN, he had already written
that a political statement engaged in by a writer-artist
"would . . . end up acknowledging, by its very nature, the ambiguity of what it's talking about." And: "There's some kind of death
that creeps into prose when you're trying to illustrate a principle,
no matter how worthy."

When writers are called on as intellectuals they are being sum-
moned not as artists, but in their idea-responding, social-reforming
capacities, exactly like politicians—or, to put it in PEN's terms,
"the state."

There at the PEN Congress, when the American poet, Allen
Ginsberg, asked the Nicaraguan writer, Omar Cabezas, about the
prolonged censorship in his country, he replied not with the grief of
a poet at the death of words, but with the defensiveness of a politi-
cian: he blamed outside pressures. Again and again one heard in
the non-writerly, ideologically anti-American comments of Gunter
Grass that he was failing to make the distinctions about the behavior of nations he would be forced to recognize in the truth of his
fictions. Many a reader of the coverage of PEN must have wondered what was so unique about *those* responses.

Did the forgers of the conference subject really mean, by intellectuals, those who stand on platforms? In that case, why not settle
for the Republican or Democratic conventions? Maybe the ideal
congerie of writer-intellectuals should include no writers at all.
Instead of balking at the appearance of a single head of state, why
not people the congress panels entirely with heads of state? All of
them have in one way or another attached their names to books,
and they could discuss government affairs without having to use
writer-middlemen at all. This organization could be called
HEADS, indicating its ideal intellectual orientation.

If what really is wanted above all is holders of passionate political views, but heads of state are still unacceptable, what about a

conference of essayists (few were represented at this one), for which the name of the organization could be changed to E. E.—essayists and editors—to be uttered in a prolonged syllable, as in screech.

"How boring!" That's what a writer whose face was ruddy with the heat of one of the more political panels exclaimed when I told him I was headed for something called "American Fiction and Poetry." It wasn't boring, it was fascinating, once you cleared the hot pepper from your palate. Here Joyce Carol Oates and Raymond Carver were trying to sleuth out for themselves and audience the difference between the impulses of poetry and fiction. When Carver described his writing poems for months or years with never a thought of stories, or stories with never a thought of poems, and wondered aloud why that might be, and said wistfully that if anyone had any insight into this "mystery" he would appreciate hearing about it, I didn't think, 'How unintellectual!' I thought, 'How writerly!'

What *was* boring, often, was the lack of real dialogue between humanists and ideologues. It is an axiom of discussion that the closer the idea-alignment of participants, the finer will be the distinctions, the more subtle the phrase and pace of thought; conversely, the greater the distance between discussants, the more will rant, cant, and slogans be hurled across the gap.

For my own part, I assume that the women who stayed away preferred to hone their ideas more finely in poems and novels. But if PEN persists in driving such writers from its congresses with crude idea-formulations, I suggest that it rename itself by adding 'I' for Intellectual. That makes it PENI. Seeming to border on the ribald, the name can be set right if we remember that it's pronounced 'penny,' as in 'penny for your thoughts.'

—1986

Her Price above Rubies

My friend B has a tighter schedule than most but has always enjoyed it. She is up at 5 A.M., runs to a jogging track on the grounds of a neighborhood school, runs there from 5:30 to 6:00 A.M., then runs home and breakfasts with her school-age children, drives to her full-time job at a school in Queens, is home in time to swim a half hour's worth of laps in a Y pool, then to supper and the evening chores of a parent and householder and the paperwork of a junior-high-school science teacher.

A minor physical impairment that would make this day impossible for her is mitigated and controlled by the adherence to the regimen of physical exercise. The necessity becomes a pleasure too; she enjoys the exercise and the first bloom of morning it reveals to her. Her body rewards her with health and stamina, and her friends have learned not to telephone after nine when she's more likely than not to be asleep.

One day while B was jogging in the dawn she felt strong arms fling themselves from behind about her neck and drag her down. At first, without thinking, she fought back. She and her assailant fell to the ground and B kept moving. A saying from her childhood sounded in her head, from the time when boys made sneering remarks about rape—"You can't thread a moving needle"—and she kept moving with all the strength of her excellent muscular body.

She screamed and fought so long and hard—rolling, kicking, biting—that it must have become clear to her assailant that he would have to kill her to prevail. Suddenly he was up and sprinting. She leapt to her feet without seeing anything about his appearance except, in one horror-struck instant, that he was a jogger too.

He ran to the lot, she to the road. As in a nightmare she knew that she had been released only to be trapped again. She would have to be swifter on foot than he in his car, which in his rage he would surely use to run her down. But she reached the road before him, encountered a woman jogging there in time to warn her from the track and saw a car race by, unidentifiable in the semidarkness of dawn.

If B had not been in fine physical shape, if she were not a runner and a swimmer, she could not have been that "moving needle." She would have been overcome. We have, alas, great evidence now; we know what can happen physically and psychically to a woman who is overcome in this way. But B got away, narrowly. How does an escape this narrow affect a life?

In B's case, this was not immediately discernible. First, her schedule had to be fulfilled. By the time she reached home, bathed, dressed, breakfasted with children, her husband was descending the stairs to begin his morning. She had barely time to tell him what had happened before she took off for work, where an early conference, the first of several in a tightly packed teaching day, was waiting.

Finally a colleague noticed her bruises, her trembling. Pressed, she told the story again, briefly, en route to another appointment. She must call the police, she was told, even though no identification was possible. She must talk about it, to someone who would understand the psychic harm.

So she telephoned her husband at his office and asked him to report the event to the police because she had no time. Nor had she time for a therapist. That evening she received a dozen guests at her house for a prewedding dinner for her oldest son, his bride- and in-laws-to-be. At odd moments she ran upstairs to her bedroom, shut the door and sobbed, then washed her face and came down again. She spoke to no one there about what had happened, for in three days her son was to be married and not only was there no time; there was also no tone of voice in which she felt it could be said.

She decided that she would not—could not—change her schedule. Or give up her beautiful mornings. Or ruin her health. Or cripple her psyche with fear. So she began to run again, same place, same time. Except of course that nothing is the same—the bloom is off the morning. She runs in fear that her assailant may wait for her, watch her, know where she lives and where her children are home alone after school. Nevertheless, she runs—with her dog, a golden retriever. We know what they are: if they had 10 tails to wag and 12 tongues to lick with, that would not be enough to show all the friendliness in their unsuspecting hearts.

"If someone jumped me," B says, "the dog would probably leap up and kiss him. But I know he wouldn't run off. I wouldn't be alone. That helps."

When I ask, like others, why she doesn't see a therapist to help her over this period, her eyes fill with tears and she answers that there's no point in taking the time since it won't help apprehend her assailant.

The shame women once felt in speaking up about rape has been largely routed. My friend is not ashamed; she hasn't the time to speak. What women set out to do they have done: they engage with the world as strenuously as men; they have banished the image of themselves as weaker beings. B knows very well that when trauma assaults the psyche anyone may become for a while, woman or man, a weaker being, deserving of shelter and respite. But she will not—cannot—stop to make her own claim on that healing. It is as if she is saying: "I've had to fight to pull the pieces of my life into some kind of balance. If I linger over this trauma everything might fall apart."

Some people say, "Running is my life," but that's hyperbole. In B's case it's true. Running is built into her schedule because there's no room for walking. She has had to run for her life and she can't stop running now.

There was a time when a woman who grew exceedingly uncomfortable in a bad situation could quietly slip from her chair in a graceful fall to the floor. In a twinkling she would be removed from a room that had grown too full of boring or offensive speakers. She was considered to have done an honorable thing—fainted—and would not be expected to return to the scene of her distress.

There was a time when a woman could grow melancholic or unaccountably invalided (one thinks at once of those nineteenth-century figures, Elizabeth Barrett or Alice James) as another form of response to unbearable situations. They paid a price, of course—melancholia and disability extract their own cost—but in an age of little real shelter for women from child-bearing and heavy domestic and social duties, even among the well-to-do, these were shelters of a kind. Within them Barrett could write poetry, James could be a memorable diarist.

Who is the modern woman? She faints not, neither does she grow melancholy. Her price is far above rubies. She keeps on running.

—1983

Low Thoughts Among the High-Minded

What is the point of a stubbornly recurring memory? Does it prod us to recoup the past in a recuperative way? "So *that's* what that meant," we say at last when consciousness lays a disentangling finger on a hardened knot of memory.

Such recognition is not always pleasing. Still, there's the relief, the release, the knot untied. Emotions about the family in which one grew up take a lifetime to unravel, and even then. . . . The school, perhaps, takes time to unravel too.

What was the woman's college I attended really like? I loved it the moment I saw it, admired high-minded female forebears, felt upheld by the nobility of the New England lives of women who had passed through before me. Yet the hardened knot of a painful moment is still tangled up in memory. Thus far there is no recouping; there are only questions.

Acres of rolling countryside—and I a city girl—with buildings scattered like outposts of nature itself; pictures of student-ancestors bending, with leg-of-mutton sleeves and long dark skirts of durable stuff, over basement laundry vats—this was Heaven to me. Those ancestor-females went on to vats of chemicals, too, and larger deeds of energy and courage. My college was one of the "Seven Sisters," proud female counterparts to the male Ivy League whose doors were shut to females. In the library women were named who once set out for teaching posts in China and India. Numbers appeared to have drowned in floods; still they kept setting out.

The example of those early women, transcending the austerity of an ill-equipped "daughters" school of the early 1800s, firing their ambition in chilly rooms, sparingly fed, seemed to release energy into the halls and onto the paths when I was there. One was going to do something oneself—even if not drown in a flood—that would be splendid. But one day something happened that made me wonder what it was I had been seeing.

We had planned an act of colorful bravado in the midst of New England austerity compounded by wartime—a dance recital for a local men's club. From a New York theater supplier the dance teacher bought loud-colored leotards (mine was yellow) and gauzy stuff for skirts.

With the dance teacher's encouragement I thought myself the most "avant" of avant-garde for my dance composed to words by Gertrude Stein: "In a ribbon, in a ribbon there is red—red, and white, and blue . . . I like shells as bells!" After reciting and running, intoning and turning, lilting and leaping, I threw myself face down into a stiff-armed fall, lifted a leg and shook it in air. If I shook long enough, I had learned, my breath crept back.

As I practiced one last shake before curtain time, another dancer with whom I had rehearsed and practiced for weeks, with whom I had shared nervousness and hope, bent to my ear. "Don't do that in front of them," she whispered. "It's like—you know—it looks like . . . you shouldn't!"

Almost standing on my head, breathless, I felt that my fellow dancer wanted me to fail, to fall, to gasp and be undone, and in a moment so near the time of performing that I could not avert or redeem it. Almost standing on my head I wondered—what is this place? Where am I? Is anything here what it seemed or is it all overturned, the opposite of what I thought?

Not in college but later I read Virginia Woolf's "A Room of One's Own," and wondered whether my school resembled less the high-minded energy of the early nineteenth-century women I so admired, and more the woman's college Virginia Woolf called Fernham, where the beef at dinner suggests "the rumps of cattle in a muddy market." And where spiritless food (at Fernham, desserts of prunes and custard; at my college a black and white pudding as tasteless as its name, "Intermarriage") bred a "dubious and qualifying state of mind." At the great university for men built on solid foundations of money to which she compares the unfortunate Fernham, fine food and wine are served. In the expansiveness of such air, the lamp in the spine lights up, says Virginia Woolf. At

Fernham—and at my college, she would have had to say had she been there—"the lamp in the spine does not light."

Yet the lamp in my spine, and in many spines, did light, because teaching was done at the highest level. Our prunes-and-custard college was to us, as Melville said of his whale ship, our Yale and our Harvard. What happened on another evening when I chaired a meeting of the political activities club bothers me not at all now, though it did then. A distinguished speaker's talk had far outrun its time limit and I attempted to conclude it, when he paused for breath, with a politeness—"We all enjoyed that so much."

"Don't interrupt, Miss," he snapped. *Miss.* Like a rap on the knuckles. What was the good of reading Plato if one was to be rapped publicly on the knuckles with Miss?

That's all right now. I've recouped it. I know what was wrong with him and with me and I've called to him down the years: "I know you have more to say, but it's not just me, it's all the others, too, those women in the leg-of-mutton sleeves bending over vats— we're all sorry, but your time is up."

The distinguished visitor didn't know about our high-minded ancestor-students, but my classmate did. Half comedy, half treachery, her act is what I cannot recoup. My mind dodges about it like a tongue over a toothache. What was it?

Was Fernham's "dubious and qualifying state of mind" to blame? Powerlessness can make attackers of the timid. Was it a narrowness and repression she brought with her? If so, Fernham didn't help her. Was it something in the atmosphere of the place as well as in her? Was it all of these? I was a quota Jew in those quota-minded days, a token presence. Was that it? Was it anti-Semitism after all, that dreariness, that dead spot in the spirit of gentiles? Was it clumsy parallel for the perfected cruelty that was at that moment going on over the ocean? Safe and far away sometimes I laugh: Oh, I must have been insufferable, choosing a hard show-off dance!

Sometimes I have thought angrily that this incident is proof that women's colleges did not ennoble minds, didn't let anyone break out of the confines of little-girl timidities or small-town bigotries. A community of women can do a great deal, but can it

alter and elevate character? What is its excuse for being? Can it
save the world? Those nineteenth-century women in leg-of-mutton
sleeves who went off to teach and sometimes to drown—*they*
thought so. Then I catch myself. I am guilty of asking for a kind of
perfection from a woman's college that is probably beyond the
capacity of any college.

Somehow we got through those dances. The men's club, fathers all, applauded kindly. Yet my dance companion continues her
drift about the stage to Tchaikovsky and the record is stuck, she
cannot get off. I am on the floor with my leg in the air and my
breath is gone. I cannot rise to say the next words. Because the
curtain never comes down, I feel I am bound one day to say suddenly, struck with insight, my foot lifted to mount a curbstone
somewhere: "So *that's* what that was!" And feel restored again to
a belief in the transcendent power of communities of high-minded
women.

—1983

Sons and Mothers

From the moment I noticed her, the woman on the platform of the suburban station looked familiar. I felt I knew her. More than that, she was someone I liked. As the train pulled in we moved together and found facing seats. With our knees companionably locked, we smiled encouragement at each other.

"I know you from somewhere." The woman opened the collar of her coat and told her names. The last had an unpleasant association. It was the family name of a teen-age boy who had assaulted my son in the playground months before. My son had been taken for emergency hospital treatment and bore a permanent scar on his leg.

She told me where she lived. Now there was no mistaking it. This was the address of my son's assailant. We had never met but we were connected. I heard my voice sounding unnaturally detached as I told her my name. My son's name. She looked astonished. But no less eager than before, she leaned toward me. She asked after my son.

"I hope he's all right now. I worried terribly. I wanted to telephone but they wouldn't let me."

I thought of how much such an encounter would have meant months before. Just as between her son and mine a connection strong as brotherhood—even if the brothers were Cain and Abel—had sprung up in a moment, so between this woman and me a terrible intimacy had once existed.

My son had gone with friends to toss a ball in the school playground. A bigger boy of sixteen rode in on a motorcycle and began to harass the group of eleven-year-olds, charging the circle and swerving away: "Gonna get you guys!"

My son and his friends had gained some playground experience: ignore bullies and they'll go away. So they went on tossing the ball. When it lobbed beyond the circle my son darted out to

169

retrieve. He was run down by the boy on the motorcycle, who gunned the motor, took aim and did not swerve.

Officer D taught the law to the eleven-year-olds: "Intention is the hardest thing to prove." The boy was charged only with driving a vehicle in a place not designated for its use and, since the motorcycle wasn't his, with driving it without a license.

My son, on crutches for weeks, tried to understand. "Why would anybody do a thing like that for no reason? Why?"

"He's sick," I said. "His mother must feel so terrible." I was trying to lessen sorrow by inventing sorrow all around.

Neighbors who knew her told us she was bringing up her family alone. A lovely woman, they said. A tragedy for her, this son who had been in trouble with the police before—drugs, assaults. The law, meant to protect juveniles from unfair prejudging, kept upholding him: he had escaped conviction every time.

Even the police report nearly succeeded in exonerating him. Conscientious Officer D, eager to avoid imputing intention, had, in wrestling words to paper, made the event look like collaboration. To appease me he amiably added a postscript: "When I stated that the injured party presented himself in the path of the motorcycle I do not mean that he brought the collision upon himself." I carried that silly victory back to the eleven-year-olds.

No one was called to the hearing. The assistant district attorney said he'd be there to present the opinion of the eleven-year-olds that the attack had been deliberate. But he had no hope of conviction. The attacker's record was by law sealed off from the judge's knowledge; the boy would be let off with a warning.

That, of course, is what happened, and the outcome further bruised the already damaged sense of justice of five eleven-year-old boys. Weeks wore by. Neighbors and families called. But the call I waited for never came. "And if she did call?" my husband asked. "What would that change?" Nothing, but it would *mean* something.

Now she, who had been so silent before, could hardly wait to talk. It was her lawyers, she explained. They would not permit her to call. "Even if I only told you I was sorry, I might prejudice my son's case. It might be taken as an admission. It was for my son. Wouldn't you have done the same?"

Wouldn't I? Could I deny her the instinctive need to protect her child, whatever form it took? By your own passion, she was saying, judge mine. I reflected on that. Hadn't I wanted to go to the hearing anyway though no witness would be called? I had fantasies of standing up and shouting till the judge was forced to hear me: "They're lying! He *intended* to hurt and might have killed!" I didn't go and I could give myself reasons. My son was healing and we wanted normalcy after upheaval. Was that cowardice? I wanted to go; I should have gone. With my hair awry, my clothes disheveled as they pulled me away, losing dignity, I ought to have gone. Part of me regrets it still.

I know a woman who, when neighborhood toughs taunted her child, ran out to hurl her rage and contempt until they grinned uneasily in their car. Then she glanced at her child, terrified by the sight of a rage-transformed mother, and stopped. She went quietly into the house with her child. In imagination I participate proudly in the moment when my friend, in her bravery, transcended every cautionary stereotype of crazed shrieking mother to do battle in the street. Yet I tremble with her, seeing the child. I understand that sudden quieting and retreat.

"Wouldn't you have done the same?" the woman on the train asked again. The child comes first, she meant. Always and always, the child comes first. But there was something wrong, and she and I both knew it.

Another and more deeply submerged feeling began to trouble her expression. I remember thinking: Whatever she says now it's too safely late. So I was unprepared for the power of it when in a low voice she added, "I wanted to call and I should have." She was quiet, without any of the earlier eager movements. She seemed to speak to herself.

"I should have called." She was staring straight ahead, not at me. "I wanted to call you, and I should have." It was as if the vision, not of sons or daughters, but of principle itself, like some phoenix heated and bright, glowed between us.

The train approached the station. Doors banged open. My companion and I stared into each other's faces as if we had only just recognized each other. When at last we rose it was as if we meant to embrace but did not. We simply acknowledged by our looking that the intimacy of sorrow would not dissolve and it hasn't, though we have never encountered each other since.

—1982

Baby-Making

Word having gotten around that I was at work on a novel about abortion, I was continually surprised by women who volunteered information about themselves. They, too, they felt I should know, had had abortions. It was never lightly said—always gravely, as if imparting a trust, yet always surprisingly, spontaneously, the pent-up information sought its own way toward release.

Sometimes the women who told were older, and the years fell away from them as they spoke, to reveal a pain still fresh. Sometimes younger, and then there was bravado: "I feel much better now!" Sometimes this was followed by a statement whose vehemence I might have thought misplaced, if I hadn't heard it so often: "I'm breaking up with my boyfriend—I've *had* it with him!"

It's a big world, and on some days so many opposing things go on, so many opposing voices are raised, that they appear to cancel one another out. The world takes on the image of a kind of Penelope-figure, weaving and unweaving, making and unmaking.

Everybody talks about the weather, Mark Twain complained, but nobody does anything about it. Nowadays, the subject of making babies seems to have replaced talk of the weather, with one great difference—everybody wants to do something about baby-making.

Since legal abortion, it seems to me, is preferable to the evils involved in either illegal abortion or the birthing of unwanted children, I am firmly prochoice. But sometimes I can sympathize with the antichoice people. A million abortions a year in America alone seems too much like another one of those sickening numbers of the twentieth century, whose speciality has been mass death.

No one wants abortions to go on and on. Everyone wishes they would end—that some honorable means could be found for a woman to maintain herself in an unmothering status if she wishes, some means to which celibacy is not the only key.

Because of all the attention lavished on the tug-of-war between pro- and antichoice forces, other aspects of the baby-making subject may have gone unnoticed—aspects that point toward proliferation of life in a way that should be satisfying to the antiabortionist, although, as it turns out, it is not. There is, for example, the California Repository for Germinal Choice in Escondido, which holds in its icy grip the frozen semen of Nobel Prize winners.

Last July, *Newsweek* reported that the first woman to make a withdrawal from the Nobel Prize-winner's sperm bank had already lost custody of two "natural" children after allegations of child abuse. The new baby daughter has already been born and a picture snapped of mother and child cheek to cheek. She and her husband have promised (threatened?) that the new "genius" will be taught alphabet and numbers before it can walk and trained on computers by the time it is three.

The famous story about George Bernard Shaw comes to mind. Approached by a woman who wished to have a child by him that would have his brains and her beauty, he replied, "But what if it has my beauty and your brains?" What punishments might this First Mother of the Spermbank care to devise for a "genius" that may not deliver?

The obvious contrast that comes to mind is with the heavy artillery that's brought to bear on abortion by antichoice forces. In the interest of the unborn child everybody feels the right to some say. Why is it that in the case of the alleged child abuser who can now take one half of her unborn child from the public domain, no one appears to have much to say?

Life magazine of November 1982 reports that in Queen Victoria Hospital in Melbourne, Australia, "donor eggs provided by third parties and fertilized by husbands are transplanted into wombs of their wives." Some of these "concepti" are frozen for future use by whoever will claim them. In the same issue, we see pictures of how, at the Eastern Virginia Medical School in Norfolk, Va., which has a waiting list of 7,000, *in vitro* babies are made. The egg is removed from the mother-to-be, fertilized in a dish by sperm from the husband and the fertilized egg later transplanted to the wife's uterus. Ten or twelve happy wives, sunning and chatting, wait their turn or rest afterward to make sure the implantation takes. But "despite a 1979 report commissioned by the Department of Health, Education and Welfare affirming the ethics of *in vitro* fertilization," *Life* reports, the United States Government has held up funding.

The church is opposed. So is Jerry Falwell. One can see why.

If procreation can be detached from lovemaking, then lovemaking can also be detached from procreation. But for most people, that has already happened, and it does not seem likely that the world will be persuaded to give up contraception.

Still—there it is. Now children can be conjured out of air, so to say. An egg can be removed from a female, placed in a dish and fertilized by extracted sperm, and the fertilized egg can be inserted—well, where? Back into the uterus of the woman who produced the egg? Or of an adoptive female who wishes to bear and rear the child? Or in a donor female body, volunteered or paid for?

Children have been born of this dish conception. The fetus has been loosed from the female. Biology may be destiny, but not in the ways anyone thought.

Nobel prize winner sperm banks, *in vitro* concepti, surrogate mothers—technology advances and as usual brings us, along with its blessings, something to offend everybody. "If God wanted sperm to be frozen," one can almost hear Jerry Falwell say, "He would have provided two pair of testicles, one regenerative and one refrigerative."

Meanwhile, in the *Radcliffe Quarterly* of September 1982, we read the news that Mother Teresa was invited to address Radcliffe's graduating seniors at Class Day. Mother Teresa, the *Quarterly* reports, "made a bid for virginity." The *Quarterly* quoted her as having said to the seniors that on "your wedding day . . . the most beautiful thing is to give a virgin heart, a virgin body, a virgin soul." The reporter, a member of the graduating class of 1983, added in straightfaced language: "Many questioned the appropriateness of the choice of Mother Teresa as Class Day speaker." All the same, Mother Teresa was heard by 20,000 people that day. Who knows where influence made its mark?

I'm not betting money that the world will go either way. Yet I do remember the young woman who told me so bravely of her abortion, which had taken, seemingly, only one day out of her life. "It was nothing—it was over like that!" She snapped her fingers.

"Just in and out of that room in minutes." Then, without my asking a question, this followed:

"I made up my mind while I was lying there—I'm going to change my life. I quit my job, I broke up with my boyfriend. I'm moving in with my parents and going back to school. No drugs, no booze. Nothing! This time I'm not going to blow it." Mother Teresa may yet get her wish, though not exactly (this is how it is with wishes) the way she wished for it.

—1982

Child Abuse

We were going to move to another state with our two small children after what was for me a lifetime in New York City. Yet I hadn't the sense to be scared. I knew no more about what I was leaving than our landlord, who would have been shocked to learn that his old apartment house represented an Eden of harmony to his tenants. Families lived there whose lives gripped other lives so that we were all—roots, rocks, trees, hills—cleft into one another like landscape.

Alone with my children in a windswept playground that was nearly empty—because in this new place, after all, everyone had backyards to be in—I saw myself with my old friend Aura again, as indeed I can now, years later, so strong was the bonding, so vivid the memory.

It is spring, the year is young, our babies are young. We are pushing those black baby carriages, our appendages, before us, mine with a booster seat on it where my daughter, the swaying rider, beats time with a shovel. We are walking along a path in Central Park and Aura's wide, duck-toed stride, open and friendly like her, precedes me for a time along a narrow path. She calls cheerfully back, "All clear!" It's our park joke, in this lovely hilly section known as the Ramble. Bird watchers walk here in spring and fall. Muggers also, sometimes, purse snatchers, male homosexuals, to pick up others the same. Also, around certain bends in the path, near a handy southern pine or other large-trunked tree, from time to time the genital exposers. Shabby, weirdly grinning men, they can sense the female approach, step forward, unzip, all in the twinkling of an eye, and have everything ready for you as you pass. Who would dare this alone?

Some rainy Sundays Aura devises arts and crafts projects; the children paint and glue macaroni elbows; Aura and I talk. She wants a second child right away. Women with education, with desire for a profession, are having their children a year, a year and a half apart, as once only the poor did.

For a few years the mother's strength will be sapped, sanity cracked and her face will look like a bowl of farina. Then one fine year all the children will be in school a full day and the mother out free for six golden hours, to read, work, go back to school, anything in the world for which she still has brains to cope. But Aura's husband won't cooperate. "He's afraid it will interfere with his work schedule. Then he'll probably decide it's all right just when I'm ready to go back to full-time work." The ridiculousness of it overcomes her and she laughs. Her beautiful brown eyes swim in their special shiny fluid and she laughs helplessly. She injects me with her laughing.

I remember my grandmother—many children, little money, and a husband whose anger could annihilate. I remember her shaking down with such laughter, putting her beyond reach. I think that such laughter must once have been the opiate of many women. Transcendent laughter. A nirvana of laughter. After such cleansing laughter we take courage to talk about how one day Aura will go back to pottery, I to writing. Or we meet in the market. Our children chase each other around the cans. We shop and talk, when we can.

Each of us knows how to deflect the other's exhausted irritation from her child. Each of us has perfected the timing needed to distract, to intercept attention, so that not every demand is directed solely toward the child's own mother. Some of the corrosive acid in the child's will is diluted, sweetened, made to harmonize a little more with what the mother can tolerate. At two, our daughters were single-purposed about toys, candy, wanting. At three, the book said, they would share.

"See the bird on the telephone wire?" "Hear the fire engine coming?" "See the garbage truck take in the spilled vegetables? Like a hippopotamus!" "Look! See! Smell! Listen!" "Two lollypops I found in my pocket just now, how about that."

Once spooning applesauce to my infant son in his feeder-seat wobbling on the table. Meanwhile placating my daughter. Hers was a simple demand: Open the plastic-domed paperweight with its snow scene locked inside.

Starting out serene as Demeter: "Mommy can't open it, darling. It's sealed. If you wait till I'm done I can find something else for you that you'll like very much."

At the utmost pitch of a crescendo of wails I smashed the paperweight against the refrigerator. Jagged bits of the brittle plastic flew everywhere and the liquid that held the snowstorm (poison?) poured over the infant feeder plate and table.

"There! Miserable! Couldn't you wait?"

And clapping my infant son to my hip, pursued her, screaming in terror, to the nursery door where I grabbed her shoulder, shook her and flung her onto the bed, her head an inch shy of cracking at the wall.

And whispered it all, in a kind of shock, to Aura next day.

"It's nothing," she said.

"Nothing?"

"The love flows over it. They forgive you."

I had read somewhere a psychologist's comment about the incidence of child abuse: inverse ratio to the proximity of the mother's female friend. When I was without one in a strange city I began to wonder what might happen, with only my husband and my children, that enclosed group that was supposed to be so holy.

I did not become a child abuser after we moved, at least no more of one than when I was a loving mother now and then erupting in my native habitat. It would be comfortable to say that after a certain time of chaos everything came right again, but the truth is, it never did. Some of the light and joy went out of child-raising because there were no loving relatives and friends to share it. Was it my fault? Was this a weak spot of dependency that moving away uncovered, like rotten strawberries at the bottom of a box beneath the top luscious layer?

I thought so then, of course, puritanically berating myself for poor "adjustment." But now I don't. We had moved to a place with many transient families. The mothers and fathers were good at adjusting. They had moved before and would again. The women, especially, had made themselves into a species of clever nomad, roaming the suburbs like Indians over the plains, locating what it took to make quick camp—doctors, dentists, pediatricians, violin and piano teachers, Girl Scouts and Cub Scouts, after-school programs, swim clubs and summer recreational care. There was nothing they couldn't find. But they never found an old friend to share child-raising with. They never found the joy Aura and I had felt on our walks through the park or on our craft days in her kitchen while the washing machine thumped and the children painted macaroni and Aura and I listened to each other's woes, then, laughing, told each other that the love would have to flow over it, what else could it do?

I don't think my seeing things this way was all my fault because once, when I got up courage enough, I asked an acquaintance in the new place whether she'd ever minded bringing up her children without extended family or old friends.

"Of course I minded at first," she said, holding on to her stoical, perfectly coping expression. "Naturally, then I got over it. But in the beginning I used to wheel my babies along the streets and the tears would roll down my cheeks. 'My God,' I'd think, 'they're so beautiful, and every little stage is so wonderful and disappears so fast. And there's no one here to see it but me.'"

—1982

The World's First Crop

When we moved our small family to a suburb of Boston, we were lucky enough to meet another family lonelier than we were. Neither the man nor the woman had any kin closer than the West Coast; ours were in New York. They had three small children. Except for them and us, they knew no one.

My heart went out to the J—'s. Through allergies, accidents, birthdays, holidays, sorrows, joys, husband-wife fights, they had no one but each other to talk to. As a family they were, collectively, an orphan. Lonely as they were, brave, full of effort and work and secret sorrow, they were reluctant at first to accept our suggestion that our two families take a week's vacation together at a small country hotel in New Hampshire in the spring. Struggling free of their dependence on self-reliance, they agreed.

Little did any of us know, greenhorns in New England, that it was black fly season in New Hampshire. We sat on the porch, swatting and trying to read. A large bulky figure, husband of the proprietor, lounged in the doorway of the wide veranda, safe behind the screen door. "They'll be with us heayah," he said evenly, "for a while."

All evening his wife was on the phone to friends. Talking about auctions in the town, about the trade, about relatives, while the guests felt their place as outsiders. The bug electrocutors, two blue lightning bolts, sizzled on either side of the porch.

The J—'s children came down with chicken pox, all three at once. Lorraine, their mother, stayed in the room with them. Her husband berated her for not knowing they had been exposed to the disease. For not knowing this was black fly season in New Hampshire. "We haven't had a sweet day between us," said Lorraine, "since we came East."

Next morning I went to keep Lorraine and her children company but found them all asleep, nestled in a blanket on the daybed. Lorraine looked exhausted, asleep on her back, eyes sunk in their sockets. The youngest child was asleep under her curved arm, his head between armpit and breast. The second child lay back against the slope of Lorraine's bent legs, his head in the blanketed hammock place between her shins. All were breathing the shallow, rasped breaths of upper-respiratory infections. All for once were peaceful, no demand made or unmet among them.

I went downstairs to the dark living room of the inn with its hard-upholstered sofa and chairs, where the proprietor was doing accounts, and asked if I could help. "But you're on vacation, dear," she said. "I feel like doing something besides reading," I answered. She pushed a folder of receipts at me. "You could put these in alphabetical order, then, if you really think so."

I began on it right away. It was quiet, with only the intermittent sound of the bug electrocutors sizzling on the porch. Through the narrow windows I could see the sunny out-of-doors. Now and then the phone rang. She answered, chatted pleasantly without letting up on her neat adding and figuring, unhurriedly continuing to enter names and amounts in a ledger.

The sun lit the upper part of Mount Monadnock, where my husband and children and Lorraine's burdened and angry husband were climbing. It also lit up the graveyard at nearby Jaffrey, where Amos Fortune, the slave who ran away from the South and turned tanner and town philanthropist in the North, lies buried. And not far from him Willa Cather, the Middle Western writer who came East to live and die.

Because we were in what was once a self-contained New England village, I thought wonderingly about the way we live now. There were villages in those days, to take people in. Or else, if the villagers were so inclined, to leave them out. But there was an in, there was an out. It was not like now, I thought, a constant flux and flow of lives—linear, linear, none with a center. Lives nowadays were lived in undulating lines like sound waves or light waves. A life could not cluster itself upon its center like a firm cabbage.

Inspiration burst upon me. I could hardly wait for Lorraine to wake up. "Our two families," I said, "ought to live together! If you're sick, we'll look after your children. When we are, you can look after ours. We'll have meals together. We won't both have to be home every day to start supper. You can enroll for the courses you want, day or evening. We'll work out a schedule, we can all have our time this way."

From her tall, spare frame, Lorraine had dropped—there was an ancient scale in the hall bathroom—four needed pounds. Her eyes were deeply circled. "We can do it. No reason not to," she answered. "We can help each other. We all need all the help we can get. There's no reason not to do it." She closed her eyes a moment. Then she said: "It's no use—I couldn't do it. I have to be the only woman in my own house. The way my mother was the only woman in hers. It's just the way it is. What good would it do to fool you?" Her eyes filled with tears. "My life will be like this till my kids are all in college."

"That's twenty years," I said.

"It's just the way my mother had to do it, too."

By the time the climbers came back from the mountain, weary and bitten, I had collected a few thoughts. When my husband collapsed on the bed and groaned, "I must be out of my mind," I announced that I had something to say. He politely allowed his eyelids to flutter while I refreshed him with the following:

"Society subsidizes the farmer, gives tax rebates to property owners. But for those who raise the world's first crop—children—there is no help. They are alone, those innocent women and men, alone with the responsibility for their children. And it may age them and embitter them and make them poor just as well as it may rejoice and enrich their lives. No matter. They are condemned to face every crisis and shoulder every burden alone. Unless they or their offspring have made some fearful mistake and broken the law. Then the state steps in to punish.

"Heads of state have cabinets to advise them," I went on. "Army chiefs of staff have aides and officers to meet with. Corporations have boards to counsel and vote on policies. But heads of families go it alone. And if the human stock goes down they're to blame, and if it ever goes up we are all damn lucky! I know the planes are all flying the other way—this is the age of the single parent, the broken family, the go-it-aloner. All the same—why shouldn't we look at where the heart is and understand that it's been wrenched from home?"

My husband was by now deeply asleep. I gazed past him and out of the window at the shining mountain.

—1983

Sometimes I Feel Like a Siblingless Child

Now that both my children have left for college I marvel at how such an inappropriate metaphor as the empty nest has taken hold. "Empty nest" is all wrong. No one has ever seen a bird mope about a nest after the departure of its young. The parent birds are off like a shot. How can a few weeks out of a spring and summer be compared with eighteen years of proximity to a child? During those years the child has grown toward adulthood; the parent has left his or her own youth behind and entered middle age.

By the time a son or daughter leaves, he or she is no longer a child for whom everything must be done but a loved companion, a person of ideas, interests, and opinions. Dearer than the most amusing house guest and far more intimate than that, what the grown, ready-to-leave-home child has become is an ideal sibling. What is more logical to say, therefore, than that what the parent of the last departing child feels is the loneliness of a newly created only child?

I grew up an only child but hardly knew it. For years I lived my after-school days and part of my evenings at my grandparents' house. It was full of children—my aunts and uncles. I knew they weren't my brothers and sisters, but I felt as if they were. My mother was the firstborn and my grandmother had gone on bearing a long time, so that my youngest aunt was only a few years older than I. In the bad old days before family planning, such things were possible—serendipitous for me if not for my grandmother.

When we moved away I became what I was—an only child. Having discovered that truth I became one with a vengeance. I read read read in my room, kept diaries, wrote stories about lonely pieces of paper blowing in the street below my window, until my mother accused me of acting like a boarder in the house.

A student of mine recently explained why she'd had to miss a class: Her daughter had left to go to college. "I know how you feel," I said. "No, you don't," she answered. Then she told me what had happened. Her daughter, a shy and studious young woman, had driven to her college at the beginning of the term and found that her roommate's boyfriend had moved into their dormitory room. Shocked and confused, her daughter had turned around and driven home again, a matter of four hours. When her mother asked why she hadn't told the roommate that such behavior was unacceptable, her daughter replied, "I couldn't embarrass her." They decided together what to do. Mother and daughter drove to school, called the roommate aside and worked it out.

The mother laughed ruefully in telling all this to me. "There was a minute there when I wished my daughter was tough enough to fight it out herself. But I guess what I did was raise the kind of person I like to have around me. She's sensitive and considerate. I'm not going to complain. God, do I miss her!"

That's it, I thought. We raise the kind of people we want to have around, and when they leave we're bound to ache at their going.

Let me be sure no one will take the sibling idea to mean I equate parenthood with palship. While my husband and I carried the burden of the full nest—feeding, clothing, teaching, reminding, guiding, nagging, yelling, and mentioning now and then that we'd had it up to here—we were parents, not siblings.

But toward the end of that span there came a moment, lasting several years, in which my son and daughter were an ideal sister and brother to me. I worked at home, and by three o'clock, when I was ready to stop, in walked this charming, witty pair. They filled my head with stories from their high-school world, did hilarious imitations that cleansed me with breathy laughter or, sometimes, groaned me their groans while I groaned them mine.

When one of them studied physics, as I had not, or when they read ahead of me in history and philosophy, they let me ask questions like a child who hasn't had a chance to study these things in school yet. When they came to the Romantic poets or Thomas Hardy's novels, there were books open on all the tables of the house. I ran up to the attic to read my college texts again. Somehow those lines from Wordsworth's immortality ode had never meant as much to me, reading them by myself for a paper, as they did now when we said them aloud to one another.

By great luck I was spared the brutalities of hard rock in the house. My sibling-children chose groups for whom language and instrument were a kind of jagged poetry.

When they played their favorite classical symphonies I relearned my own. All through my lonesome adolescence I had played Brahms in my room (a noisy boarder) until my parents were sure it was the music that was making me sad. It was the opposite. I was sad and the music provided a corridor along which I could let my emotions out for a promenade before it was time to shut them up again. By adulthood I had sickened of Brahms' Second Symphony. Not that its tonalities were too obvious, like Tchaikowsky's, but that it was too filled with me, and I couldn't bear to hear it now that I didn't have to. But when my son called me into his room one day to hear a gorgeous record he had just brought home, I was able to listen to Brahms' Second cleansed of my infusions—gorgeous indeed and, to my astonishment, full of stoic courage.

I didn't feel that my learning time was over. I could have gone on and on. But our children had to leave. First my daughter, taking with her most of the ideas of Western civilization, along with yoga, modern dance, gossip and tea in the kitchen, meandering bicycle rides through unfamiliar leafy neighborhoods.

Two years were left with an imaginative and well-read son in the house. Precious they were, but with a drop of poison in them. Alarmed to find himself a sudden only child, he began to withdraw a little from us and we from him. We knew what was coming.

At the end of a Saul Bellow novella, the protagonist cries at the funeral of an unknown man. He has had nowhere to put his grief, yet knows he is right to have it. Maybe that's what we're supposed to do, he thinks—to acknowledge and to mourn.

Not a popular sentiment for Americans, who like to think that mental health can help you beat the rap on grief. But the truth is that some sadnesses have no cause but in our humanity and no cure but in our bearing them.

My sadness at my children's leaving is well mixed with my joy at their being ready to go, my pride in them for the courage and love they show to us in their going.

And so I tell friends: If you think you see me now and then look as if something's missing from my life, let me refer you to this feeling every parent with luck will know—this joy of siblings. After such children leave home, is it any wonder if some times you feel like a siblingless child?

—1982

An Immoral Tale

My aunt tells the story of a woman of her generation who, in the Depression thirties, perpetrated an extraordinary hoax, even for those desperate times. She was clever and young and energetic, also poor and with few prospects. Her fiancé having abandoned her in early pregnancy, she set out to locate, among the obituary listings, details about some freshly widowed childless gentleman who was rich. Her pregnancy was not yet at the dreaded stage of "showing." Hastily she put her pennies together, bought a new dress and a bouquet of flowers and, wearing the one and carrying the other, presented herself at the door of a bereaved older gentleman whom she had never seen or heard of before.

She threw herself upon his bosom. A dear friend of his wife's, she sobbed. She embraced him in sorrow. She insisted that he allow her to prepare a comforting meal for him. She urged him to pull himself together for his darling wife's sake. She drew him out for walks in the park, holding tightly to his arm. Very soon, she married him.

My aunt tells this story with distaste, but adds judiciously, "She was a faithful wife. He always believed her child was his own, premature." And when he died—presumably a happy man—he left his wealth to his clever, faithful wife and her son.

There it is, nearly a moral tale after all. A victimless crime that ends with something for everyone. True, it leaves a shuddery after-effect. The dead first wife might have to return like Fruma-Sarah in "Fiddler on the Roof" to haunt the living. My aunt gives the whole affair, after this many years, a grudging nod. That's how far women had to go for survival in those days. Without a husband—a protector, a meal ticket, a father for one's child—life's gates locked shut against you.

My aunt and I have no difficulty in agreeing here. Where we

run into trouble is with instances of daring by contemporary wom-
en. By the woman, for example, who is pregnant and unmarried
and teaching in a school on Long Island. For her my aunt cannot
summon even grudging approval. She finds her wrong on every
count—for deliberately bringing a fatherless child into the world,
for failing to be discreet about it and for insisting on her right to
teach children throughout all this. The young, believes my aunt,
deserve comfortable years in the midsection of societal mores while
they get their bearings; they don't need a teacher on society's cutting edge.

Unlike my aunt, liberal friends say that of course the pregnant
unmarried teacher on Long Island ought not to be fired. Yet even
they seem troubled by the publicity, and wonder whether she might
not have taken a leave when she "got big." It appears that there's a
shuddery aftereffect here, too. Neither side denies that a woman is
better off being able to work and support her child instead of
having to lie and cheat her way into marriage like that woman in
the hoax-story of the thirties. What both liberal and conservative
views seem to agree on is that "discreetness" is the missed quality
here.

Springing from the root, "to discern," the word "discreet"
itself reminds us of the connection between good judgment and
prudence—a concept one hardly cares to refute. Unless one steps a
little to one side and tries to make out what it is that discretion in
this instance might have kept us from discerning.

In the case of the schoolteacher on Long Island, the once dreaded "showing," that epiphany of sexuality that descends on wom-
en alone, is compounded by the publicness of teaching, an even
intenser showing-forth. It is this showing that in the past most
surely led women to punishment and death. Only think of Hester
Pryne's pariah-life, a scarlet A emblazoned on her bosom, a baby
in her arms. Think of the old ballads. Why is Mary Hamilton
riding to the gallows? She has slain her own dear babe whose birth,
though conceived of "the highest Stuart of all," has shamed her. It
is the stuff of the old vaudeville plays, so painfully true that it had
to be exaggerated into melodrama: daughter shivering in doorway
with baby in arms, while father points the way into the snowstorm.
These women did not flaunt, yet they could not hide. This act of
showing is now boldly reclaimed. By choosing this formerly de-

spised condition, a woman has gained control and dominance over it.

If the angry ghost-wife haunts the hoax-story of the thirties, think of the ghostly throngs that cluster about the story of the teacher on Long Island: Mary Hamilton and Faust's Gretchen and Tess of the D'Urbervilles and a million nameless others. These wretched spirits of destroyed women come back not in anger or revenge, but to cry, "Redeemed!"

My aunt and I cannot budge each other on this matter. Each of us is in her own way right. She is of a generation that takes with deep seriousness society's disapproval, as well she might: women have died of society's judgments in such things. Yet even here there are a few jokes. Society's response to sex is no less funny than any other part of the human comedy. My aunt, who monitors talk shows, reports, for example, that the teacher on Long Island was asked by a radio interviewer why, if she wanted a baby but wasn't married, she didn't use artificial insemination. The technique thought by some to be an abomination can, when convenient, appear to be worthier of respect than the natural act.

Two memories intervene here. One is of those ignorantly prurient conversations we used to have as very young children, before sex education got to us, about how you "did it." I remember the judicious surmise of a doctor's daughter, an exceptionally clean child, who solemnly stated that "it" was done with a piece of cotton. And one day on a crowded Manhattan bus my daughter, then five years old, chose to ask the question about sex we parents had been told to be on the lookout for. She said she remembered about how the baby gets out. What she'd forgotten was how the baby gets in. Answer it when it comes, the child psychologists advise, or the child will think you disapprove and may never ask again.

Straphangers crowded where we sat. I had the impression that those whose woolen hats prevented their hearing my explanation were supplementing with lip-reading. At least, I thought, sweating in too much outdoor clothing in the overheated bus, I am not abetting ignorance or distortion. To my mortification, my daughter broke into giggles. Had I raised a child who sniggered at sex? Soon she made clear why she laughed: "That's a funny joke, Mama. Now tell me the truth."

Sometimes I like to think I can be as quick to see a ludicrous situation as even a fresh-minded five-year-old. What's the solemnity about? Then I remember that pageant of punished women.

Let us give thanks to women of boldness who do what they must in every generation. Though they sometimes make us shudder, it will be owing to them if society ever turns a less demonic face toward the humanity of its daughters.

—1983

William Faulkner and the Art of Ruthlessness

I remember how she looked on the TV screen—a perfectly groomed, calm-voiced woman. Her softly Southern tones were controlled and even, betraying no tremor of the internal shock her father's words must have produced in her.

She was William Faulkner's daughter, and, she was saying, one day she made a request that meant a great deal to her. She had seen in her father certain signs that meant one of his periodic drinking bouts was coming on. Her birthday—her thirteenth, it may have been—was coming, and she wanted her father to be his right self for it. I am recalling her words from the televised interview, but I think I am close. "Daddy," she said, "please don't drink."

About Faulkner's response I know I must be right because it still chills my bones.

"No one remembers Shakespeare's child," he said.

We understand at once what happened. Instead of answering "I can't" or "I won't," Faulkner replied by pointing to his status outside his relationship with his daughter: "I am Shakespeare. What have I to do with you?"

Account for it by the fury of the alcoholic whose drink is interfered with. By the panic of the father who sees pride and disguise pierced by a young girl. What is left is still the nearly intolerable vision of a grown man lifting a boulder to smash a child.

What is the nature of this boulder? Figments, dreams, fantasies, visions—the most delicate stuff in the world created it: the boulder is art.

I won't argue whether Faulkner is our Shakespeare; that's not the point here. What is is that I can't imagine the American novel without Faulkner, nor do I want to. I can't argue, either, whether

193

Faulkner really needed drink to write; he felt he did, and what he
felt he needed was iron law to him. Artists may vary the law with
the need—gambling, sex, risk, invalidism, the allurements of the
underworld.

This ruthless ability to wrest what's needed from society is part
of our understanding of what makes the artist. Would Faulkner
have written better, more, if he'd said yes to his daughter that day?
Impossible question. The sum of a great artist's life, greater than its
parts, has as well a greater retrospective inevitability than our own
ordinary-mortal lives. Art cannot be "done in" by biography (look
at Pound, look at Céline) or rescued by it. It stands—ruthless,
boulderlike, alone. That is perhaps its fascination for us: that
flawed mortals create something that outwits mortality. "I have my
statues against the sky," said Virginia Woolf.

Crueler than Reaganomics is the harsh economy of the history
of art. What doesn't rise goes under. Not only does no one remember Shakespeare's child; no one remembers whole rosters of
would-be Shakespeares. They too may have scalded their children
with words like Faulkner's, but their names are as blotted as those
of their unhappy offspring.

Could things be any other way? Can we imagine, for example,
attending an art show at the Whitney that is described thus:

"The artist, while at work on these rather poor paintings, was
making, according to the testimony of his children (slide show at 6
P.M.), heroic efforts on their behalf."

Would we want to?

And yet, and yet—must we impute what we do impute to those
who don't fully flower? Is there a way of looking at certain artists
that is closer to what one might call, up-to-dately, "holistic"?

I told a friend about a fine musician I know who does not give
recitals. In order to perform she would have had to tour, and she
has a young son who wouldn't eat when she was gone. When that
phase was over, her husband became ill. She was stuck. She gave
lessons and played for her friends at home.

"More likely," my friend said, "she used all that as an excuse
and never had the drive or the passion to be a performer."

Perhaps—in the Reaganomics view of art. From the holistic
one, it may be that the very qualities that made this woman a

musician would have been killed off by the ruthlessness needed to become a performer under such conditions.

Memoirs by children of creative dynamos often show us how, emotionally, they step back to tell us of their pain, which is less their pain than a moment in their parent's biography. They learned not to make the extravagant claims of love. A certain mentalness flattens their accounts. Perhaps they were, at last—those who were not destroyed by Niagara—bored by it.

Recently I attended a memorial service, arranged by her children, for a woman who had been a painter. She was an artist who never achieved fame. She had been married to a man with a flourishing triple-pronged career—novelist, editor, teacher. She had moved to places congenial to his work, had raised several children, had been hostess at social gatherings and had painted. At last, when her husband was near retirement from his numerous jobs and honorary appointments, all of which had for so long infused him with energy, she had said, "Now I want a life that's right for me."

She was by choice a painter of wilderness who had had to live in cities and suburbs. At last they moved to a remote house on a hilltop, glassed all around, where sunrise and sunset, mountains and ocean were in daily view. But soon after, her husband died. She had waited to begin her real life as an artist and could not turn back now. Those last years in the remote hilltop house must have been lonely. Yet in the time left to her, before she herself became ill, she had her first experience of working as a full-time artist in an environment of her choosing. In the volume of work produced, and the inner security with which she lived in those last years, there is testimony to the determination, strength and vision of a complete artist.

The children said it was a memorial for their mother, and of course it was that. I thought it was also a memorial for an artist who had refused to be ruthless in the name of work. The price she paid for that refusal seemed almost palpable, in the lack of awards, honors, shows, except where local, bestowed by neighbors and community.

"What shall we do with Mama's paintings?" her children asked, embarrassed by their love of their mother's work, wanting to show that of course they understood—no one would want them.

I wish I knew the answer. They are not boulders, not statues against the sky. Softer and more perishable, mutable like us, they are perhaps the mulch on which our humanity grows.

—1982

The Luck of the Trip

Even in these days of easy access, foreign travel can still hold something of the mysterious and the magical: the unaccustomed can release soundings from the deep. "For the world . . . ," in Matthew Arnold's words, is "so various, so beautiful, so new. . . ." Yet it is the same world that is "Swept with confused alarms of struggle and flight."

Various kinds of luck go with us when we travel, little seeming miracles along the way, if luck is good. I don't mean only the lugubrious miracle of a canceled ticket on a plane that later flies out carrying a terrorist's bomb. I mean simpler ones too, like a historic house kept open beyond regular hours on just the day your tour bus arrives late. There's also bad travel luck, of course. You arrive at the museum the week it's shut for repairs.

The luck of the trip, the serendipity of it, or its opposite, frustration and the feeling of being shut out, can flavor memories the way, for some of us, spices do a meal.

One summer my husband and I spent some highly flavored days in a tiny village in East Lothian, a province in the Lowlands of Scotland in view of the Lammermuir Hills, site of literary mystery and romance.

Not far from our inn stood a great Scottish estate that during World War II had been turned into a school for Jewish refugee children. It had provided blessed safety to a lucky few in an encroaching world of terror. We were going there for my husband's first adult return.

A taxi from the neighboring town of Dunbar brought us along a winding road at the end of which the broad-winged mansion still stood ("It seems like a miracle," my husband said) amid parklike acres bordered by forest.

We peered through the massive groundfloor windows at first in delight, then in awful disappointment, as my husband saw that all the rooms were bare. The whole place was locked and empty, about to be sold.

As we stood wondering what to do next, out of the forest, as in a fairy tale, came a beautiful young woman in full riding habit, astride an enormous horse. After a few moments of conversation she said she knew the caretaker well, and galloped off to fetch him.

In what seemed miraculously little time (the driver from Dunbar meanwhile leaning against his car and watching with sympathetic interest), a sprightly gray-haired man of about sixty arrived. He opened the mansion, marched us up the stairs to the great rooms—even helping my husband identify the specific master bedroom that had been his dormitory—and down to the cavernous kitchens. My husband gazed at the great fireplaces. One of his jobs had been to build the fires. Then, while I photographed from below, the caretaker took my husband scampering over the rooftops so he could look down at the broad and sunny countryside.

The return to this estate caused floods of memories in my husband. We went back for many more visits, and he walked the orchards and fields and gazed his fill at the stones of the house.

My husband also wanted to see, at last, the surrounding countryside that had been unknown to him at that school in wartime. After our encounter with the young woman and the caretaker, we were ready for Scottish serendipities everywhere. Soon another one was offered that might have provided at least a small album of mementos. Were we mistaken not to follow luck a second time?

Our inn included a comfortable pub whose Scottish host was warmly responsive to the purpose of our trip. No doubt thinking we needed some restorative, he urged on us our first taste of single-malt whisky. Amid the dark woods and gleaming brasses of the pub, we sampled the fortifying native brew.

Mismatched gustatory pair though we are, my husband and I ate in peace before the fire in the dining room. His taste for plain cooking was fulfilled, and our host joked that he would pour onto my food all the spices and dressings he left off my husband's. Young Scottish waitresses in tartan skirts, as if in sympathy with what we ordered, blended sauciness and straightforwardness. Indeed, one of our pleasures was to listen to the tough coquetry of their banter with the gentlemen who dined singly at their tables, the "travelers" for which the inn was a mainstay.

After dinner one night we fell into conversation with one of the Scottish travelers, as interested in our being Americans as we in his being Scots. If we were still at this place when he swung round again, he said, he'd bring along his Highland family tartan.

Hour after hour the traveler drank the recommended drink of our host while we sipped coffee, talked, read brochures, and planned excursions. We thought of going to see the oldest existing dovecote (pronounced doocut), pictured standing alone, conical, like some ancient magician's hat flung upon the landscape. A picturesque thirteenth-century castle ruin could be come upon by walking along the towpath of the Tyne River. It had an authentic dungeon, an oubliette, whose tiny air-grid was pressed into the courtyard stones underfoot, a horror from the past.

The Scottish traveler remarked that it would be an awful shame—he moved his arm wide for emphasis and nearly toppled his glass—if we didn't go out to the moors to see the heather. "Oh, the blooming purple heather!" I cried, literary memory stirred.

Well, no, our Scotsman answered, it wasn't the right season for it to be purple, more like a dried brown, but better to see it now than not at all. He offered to take us out in his car next day and I was about to accept with heartfelt thanks when my husband called me aside.

"Have you noticed how much of that malt whisky he's been taking in? And he starts at lunch."

I had noticed, but I argued all the same. What could happen if his car did weave a bit out on the moors? Whom could we hit? Cathy and Heathcliff? That was a different moor. I could hear myself sounding like a child wanting something so much that no impediment feels real. At last I had to admit that a trip with an imbibing driver, even a charming Scotsman with his own tartan, even to the moors, could cause me more anxiety than pleasure.

Lucky and unlucky, in one moment! It wasn't in any way the same order of things, or meaning, or weight as the disappointment of peering in at the windows of the locked and empty house. My husband's return to the rescuing school was deeply important to both of us, and I'd have done anything to help insure its success.

Yet I could feel at this moment the sharp pang of a different kind of adventure missed because it had no luck.

Where was my horsebacked rescuer? As soon as one arrived we would be on the moors. Not in a heavy-engined modern automobile that can roar along at ninety miles an hour and kill or maim every living thing before or in it, but in an old touring car, the closest thing to a horse and buggy with pistons.

We would weave among the intoxicating heather all in purple bloom now (why not?) and heady with the smell of a Scottish spring. Proceeding at a scythe's pace, the Scottish traveler, kilted, and whistling a jaunty Scottish air, his vision unblurred by drink, commands the wheel. His belt and sporran lie across his lap, coming to rest on his right hip like Orion's buckler, his brave kneecaps bare above the thistle-embroidered bands of his argyle socks. It's a remarkable sight, considering that I never saw it.

When the historic house is locked, when circumstance conspires against us, the mystery of travel luck shapes itself into questions. Why does fate bring us at such a moment to this place instead of that one? Why does this door swing open and that one stay shut? And why does the missed trip (is it lucky or unlucky to have missed it?) grow rich life of its own? There it is, architect of inner vision, forming spires and turrets in the mind.

—1990

3. Celebrations

"Wadja Geffa Christmas, Li'l Boy?"

Once upon a time, at that darkest season of the year that strikes so dismally on the soul that humankind since its beginning has been impelled to light lights, tell stories, come together in reverence as well as revelry, and in general do everything it can to dispel gloom and encourage optimistic attitudes, I found myself in a Woolworth's with my six-year-old son a few days after Christmas.

Tinsel festooned the ceilings. Santa balloons dangled at the crossroads of the aisles. Christmas candies crowded their brilliance behind counters. An artificial tree, propped on a bit of green carpet strewn with empty gift boxes, winked its beckoning light bulbs.

It was beside this tree that a stranger approached my son.

He was drunk, but because of the season euphemisms came to mind: He was tipsy; he was tiddly; he had dipped too deep in the wassail bowl. The condition of his coat indicated that he had lain not long before in some unclean place.

Swaying, he mumbled, "Wadja geffa Christmas, li'l boy?"

My son threw an imploring glance in my direction. A shy six-year-old sees the world as an ambush of adults, all waiting to step out and zing him with a question: "How do you like *school?*" "What's your teacher's *name?*" "What did you get for Christmas, little boy?" seemed to strike him as of that order.

I could at that moment have moved in brightly and said, "We have our own wonderful holidays!" But some stubborn silence came over me, along with a kind of curiosity generally considered too cruel for mothers. I wanted to see what would happen.

At last my son mumbled to the mumbler, "Nothing."

The drunk, who had been so eager to impart to his usual condition the legitimacy and benevolence of holiday season cheer, was flabbergasted. He swayed as if he might topple, crash, into the tree. "Oh, you poor little boy!"

The same answer flabbergasted a young college student from the Midwest who lived with us for a time. When she learned that we were bringing up young children in a Christmasless home she reacted as if I had withheld vital nourishment from the family fare.

"It's a holiday of love and sharing," she said, heartstruck. "How can you not participate in that?"

When we watched the dramatization on TV of the beloved Dickens story, "A Christmas Carol," I felt that she must be stealing covert looks at me. I felt her transforming me into Scrooge, the bitter old skinflint who says "Bah, humbug!" to Christmas and who has stepped from the pages of Dickens to become a symbol, forever, of the hardened heart that even Christmas can't move.

Who else is it in our culture, besides Scrooge, who doesn't observe Christmas?

I wonder whether some graduate student might at this moment be working out in a dissertation a link between Dickens's Scrooge and Shakespeare's Shylock. After all, he is a kind of Shylock figure, isn't he—Scrooge? With his isolation and his bitterness and his trust only in commerce and gold that cannot touch the heart?

It is hardly Dickens's fault if the Shylock figure is already there, planted by Shakespeare in the collective unconscious, ready to cast his outcast's reflection on Scrooge, who in turn casts it upon whoever, like him, does not celebrate Christmas.

The end of "A Christmas Carol" is general rejoicing. Scrooge, having been shown the terrors he escaped by his conversion to Christmas, is thankful.

Toward the end of Shakespeare's "A Merchant of Venice" comes a searing, scathing exposure on all sides. Shylock the trapped Jew—trapped by society into avarice, trapped by avarice into the horror of his revenge—appeals for recognition of his human but separate existence. Portia, the Christian judge, delivers her "the quality of mercy" speech, then mercilessly strips everything from Shylock, who suffers enforced conversion.

I know a Jewish couple who prefer to celebrate Christmas rather than Hanukkah with their children, and for pretty much the same reasons that our student from the Midwest offered. When a whole country is ringing out its bells, some Jewish families think it wise to become Christmas converts. Having "laundered" this holiday into images of Victorian England, whose very centerpiece is "A

Christmas Carol," they must then make sure they are not cast into the role of Scrooge.

As if the glory of America were not its pluralism. As if the scorched old melting pot had not long since been discarded, but was boiling again in the midst of midwinter, boiling down diversity, making the many into the few.

What is Hanukkah but the symbol of the few against the many? What does it confront us with but the fight for Jewish identity as well as physical survival? What can it remind us of in our post-Holocaust era but the threat of the annihilation of Jews and the astonishing existence of an ongoing Jewish people?

Although the victory in 165 B.C. of a small band of rebels, the Maccabees, over a king who demanded the conversion of Jews to Zeus worship seems miracle enough, there is more. Hanukkah commemorates also the lamp oil in the temple that is said to have been sufficient for only a single day but that burned for eight. During the holiday a candle is added at each evening's candle lighting. At last eight candles, plus the one that lights the others, all blaze up like the miracle of memory itself.

A devout woman helped care for our children a few days a week while I was out at work. Whenever a Christian holiday came around I would wish her joy in it. With great sensitivity, knowing that we were Jews, she would ask each time what it was that she ought to say to us in return. She meant that she could not automatically toss the greeting back—"You have a merry Christmas, too."

It also most touchingly meant that she wanted to wish us joy in something, if only she knew what it could be. We took to figuring things out on the calendar together. Before Christmas we'd say that in so-and-so many days she could wish us a happy Hanukkah. At Easter there was Passover not far ahead or behind. She was happy to hear it. She could receive our greeting and give one too.

The Talmud speaks of a contention between two schools concerning the kindling of the menorah. One school urged a burst of light from all eight candles at once, then the reduction night by night of their number until one burned alone. The view of the opposing school, I am happy to say, prevails. It held that in matters of holiness there can be no dwindling. Start with one, says this school—for the light must increase.

—1982

Reclaiming

The way they tell it in my family, at first there *was* no Hanukkah. My immigrant grandparents, once pious, felt overwhelmed, it seemed, by six children clamoring for melting-pot America. In December, presents were exchanged. It wasn't Christmas, but it wasn't Hanukkah either. The calendar obliged: it juxtaposed, or even overlapped, the holidays.

Assimilation? Hardly. The family dinner was likely to be pot roast and potato pancakes, called by their Yiddish name, latkes. Slippage. What happened after that is the story of how an immigrant family, by its third generation, reclaimed traditions abandoned in its first.

One aunt married a more religiously observant man; then another did, and then I did. By the time my children were born, Hanukkah was firmly in place. Not just traditional food and presents at the right time, but candles in a menorah for eight days, songs and spinning the dreidel, at which my husband had excelled as a boy. And the story of Hanukkah: how the Maccabees led a band of Jews in revolt against enforced conversion to Hellenic gods, and won, despite great odds. When a cruse of sacramental oil sufficient for one day was lit in the rededicated Temple in Jerusalem, it burned, the story goes, for eight.

My husband's memories from his Vienna boyhood became part of our children's. His are simple and straightforward: the blessing of the Hanukkah candles, each night one more added to the menorah and illuminated, until at last all eight blaze at once; the giving of Hanukkah gelt, small amounts of money, to the children to bet on the outcome of dreidel-spinning.

Our two streams blended in the children, and the children's memories are now also mine: They light the candles, which in turn illuminate me.

My husband taught the blessings and the songs to all of us together. I fumbled at the piano, sight-reading while we sang, loud, to cover the mistakes. "Maoz Tzur" ("Mighty Rock"), and whatever else seemed appropriate from a secondhand songbook for religious festivals. My mother flung herself into making latkes, cheering on her grandson, who hung around the stove, an appreciative gobbler-up of delicious pancakes hot and crisp from the frypan.

My mother knows the secret of keeping potatos snowy white throughout their tedious, knuckle-skinning preparation on the grater (no blender or food processor for her: texture is everything). Hers don't blacken. Mine do, just as matzo balls, when I'm foolish enough to try them on Passover, explode as soon as put to boil in the pot, making the cooking water resemble a kind of kosher egg-drop soup. (When you're good at reverse cooking alchemy, as I am, you have to be careful where you lay your hands on holidays whose message is transcendence.)

Later, we had the good fortune to be invited as a family to a neighboring family's Hanukkah zimria, a songfest. Though the food was always good, the thrilling center of it was the communal singing. These friends had gathered and copied for their guests a treasure of songs, well beyond "I Had a Little Dreidel." We sang them in parts and rounds to the accompaniment of a piano, a guitar, and finger cymbals passed around so that even the most unmusical could take a turn at clopping out the rhythm. The host's gorgeous baritone (in his pre-parent days it had graced the Christmas programs of the Collegiate Chorale) led the motley enthusiasts.

In Hebrew school the children made menorahs. Let my sons's words describe his: "A yam-shaped slab of clay into which I poked holes with a pencil, then slathered on gold paint. I considered it a work of art." So did I. And we managed to use it alongside our store-bought menorah year after year (as we used my daughter's blue-and-gold-painted clay candleholders on Friday nights) without burning down the house.

The children are now grown. My daughter, playing over Hanukkah memories, lists as favorites the candle-lighting, singing, and dreidle-spinning. Conspicuously omitted are the eight days of present-giving. I think I know why. Some sense must have seeped through of our wondering what on earth to give the children—every night a present?—after the second or third. She spotted the real and separated it from the false, even though we stopped this routine when the children were big enough to appreciate a single gift on the first night alone.

My son, however, remembers that on one of those multiple nights he received a present for which he had "a true hungry desire": a sort of machine that heated up plastic squares to make dinosaurs pop out. He played with that toy for weeks or months (he seems to think it went on for years—a mystical megalosaurian experience). Would I have wanted us to pass that up? Of course not. The senses are memory's mulch, and the dinosaur trail leads back to the meaning of Hanukkah lights as surely as Proust's tea-dipped madeleine leads back to love.

I've called my husband's Hanukkah memories simple. They are not. His parents were caught in the Holocaust. At fourteen, he escaped Vienna on a children's transport, and never saw his parents or home again.

My husband remembers that in his family the dreidel was homemade, a scrap of metal baked in the oven. What's a dreidel? It's a top with a spinning-point below and a grasper-point above. In between is a four-sided body, each side bearing a Hebrew letter—nun, gimel, hay, and shin—an acronym for the Hebrew sentence: "Nes gadol hayah sham": "A great miracle happened there." Spin it and bet on the outcome—which of the four letters will fall face up?

Is this encouraging gambling in the young? Perhaps. But neither our children nor those of friends have become gamblers. (Thus far, one must always say, a form of knocking wood, and what's wrong with a very small hedge against the evil eye, which is so very large?) Maybe there is something about sharing a bit of gambling in a lit-up family celebration that takes away the urge to indulge that impulse elsewhere. I hope so.

We combined. Between us we reclaimed Hanukkah: my husband from a murderous time of madness in Europe, I from a family in America comfortably going down forgetfulness road. A branch of the family that might have seeped through the cracks of time and sifted itself out of Jewish memory entirely somehow has renewed and extended itself (thus far) into a Jewish future. Like the original cruse, which had oil for only one night yet burned for eight, we have managed to rekindle ourselves.

Perhaps here is a clue to the connection between gambling and Hanukkah. Wasn't the whole thing a gamble? Against great odds? Isn't survival always a gamble, and the survival of the Jews in this century the greatest gamble of all? What are the odds on miracles?

My husband showed our children how to spin the dreidel, and then, giving the whole thing an extra bravura dimension, how to flip it upside down to make it land on its head, where it continues its spinning. If that isn't against all the odds, I don't know what is.

—1986